Message from the Secretary

The President's Fiscal Year 2016 Budget Request of $41.2 billion for the Department of Homeland Security reflects our continued commitment to ensuring a homeland that is safe and secure.

A safe and secure homeland is one in which the liberties of all Americans are assured, privacy is protected, and the means by which we interchange with the world—through travel, lawful immigration, trade, commerce, and exchange—are secured.

The security of our Nation will continue to be tested by new and emerging threats. Through the tremendous dedication, focus, and professionalism of the Department's workforce, and the resources requested by the President and Congress, we will address such challenges head-on.

The FY 2016 Budget focuses resources on key capabilities in each of our mission areas. These include: preventing terrorism and enhancing security, securing and managing our borders, enforcing and administering our immigration laws, safeguarding and securing cyberspace, and strengthening national preparedness and resilience.

Sincerely,

Jeh Charles Johnson

Table of Contents

Fiscal Year 2016 Overview

	FY 2014 Revised Enacted	FY 2015 President's Budget	FY 2016 President's Budget	FY 2016 +/- FY 2015
	$000	$000	$000	$000
Total Budget Authority:	$ 60,417,017	$ 61,125,061	$ 64,858,484	$ 3,733,423
Less: Mandatory, Fee, and Trust Funds:	(10,826,987)	(11,987,538)	(12,909,477)	(921,939)
Gross Discretionary Budget Authority:	**49,590,030**	**49,137,523**	**51,949,007**	**2,811,484**
Less: Discretionary Offsetting Fees:	(3,526,605)	(4,505,990)	(4,042,340)	463,650
Net Discretionary Budget Authority:	46,063,425	44,631,533	47,906,667	3,275,134
Less: FEMA Disaster Relief - Major Disasters Cap Adjustment:	(5,626,386)	(6,437,793)	(6,712,953)	(275,160)
Less: Rescission of Prior-Year Carryover - Regular Appropriations:	*(543,968)*	-	-	-
Adjusted Net Discretionary Budget Authority:	39,893,071	38,193,740	41,193,714	2,999,974

Fiscal Year 2016 Budget Request
U.S. Department of Homeland Security

The Department of Homeland Security's (DHS) ultimate mission is to secure the Nation from the many threats we face. This requires the dedication of nearly a quarter million employees with responsibilities that range from facilitating the efficient flow of commerce; preventing terrorism; protecting our national leaders; securing and managing the border; enforcing and administering immigration laws; and preparing for and responding to disasters. Our duties are wide-ranging, but our goal is quite clear—*keep America safe*.

The complex mission of securing the homeland and protecting the American people can only be accomplished with appropriate resources to support the Department's diverse and wide-ranging programs. The Fiscal Year (FY) 2016 Budget is grounded in the Secretary's strategic vision of a DHS that operates with an enhanced unity of effort across the Components that comprise DHS. Enhancing DHS unity of effort will enable the Department to best fulfill its mission responsibilities in service to the Nation. Consistent with this strategic vision, the FY 2016 President's Budget will help to strengthen DHS's existing business processes, develop new ones in areas of need, update the organizational structure, and re-orient and bolster a number of command and control functions. Concurrent with the FY 2016 President's Budget, DHS is providing a blueprint for a new Common Appropriation Structure to the Congress, which if adopted would standardize the manner in which Components within DHS plan, program, budget, and execute their resources beginning in FY 2017. This will help DHS ensure future threats are met by front-line personnel that are fully trained, equipped, and supported.

In keeping with the theme of operating a more efficient and effective Department, the FY 2016 Budget continues its support of the President's Management Agenda and Cross-Agency Priorities introduced in the FY 2015 President's Budget. These reform priorities are focused on four key areas: effectiveness, efficiency, economic growth, and people and culture. Notably, the FY 2016 President's Budget includes key investments intended to prepare our Nation for the effects of climate change, and secure the federal civilian government information technology enterprise. The Budget also continues investment in the Department's Financial Systems Modernization initiative, intended to modernize legacy financial systems, improve the quality of financial information to support decision making, and provide timely and accurate reporting.

To create additional flexibility to fund essential DHS operations, the FY 2016 President's Budget reflects near-term efficiencies identified through process improvements and overhead savings by eliminating unfilled vacancies, using Voluntary Early Retirement Authority and Voluntary Separation Incentive Payments, and reducing wireless communication costs, among others. Furthermore, DHS prioritized its essential programs and core capabilities to provide the most critical tools necessary for the Department to carry out its missions and responsibilities to keep our Nation safe.

FUNDING PRIORITIES

The FY 2016 Budget for DHS is $64.9 billion in total budget authority, $51.9 billion in gross discretionary funding, $41.2 billion in net discretionary funding, and $4.0 billion in discretionary fees. As part of total DHS funding, $6.7 billion for the Disaster Relief Fund (DRF) is provided separately from discretionary amounts, pursuant to the *Budget Control Act of 2011.*

The Budget focuses resources on key capabilities in each of the Department's mission areas: prevent terrorism and enhance security, secure and manage our borders, enforce and administer our immigration laws, safeguard and secure cyberspace, and strengthen national preparedness and resilience.

Prevent Terrorism and Enhance Security

Protecting the American people from terrorist threats remains DHS's highest priority. Safeguarding critical infrastructure and implementation of layered security on land, in the air, and on the sea are essential to combating any terrorist threat. The Department has prioritized investments in technology and risk-based, intelligence-driven programs like the Transportation and Security Administration's (TSA) Pre✓™ and Global Entry, and in the assets necessary to carry out DHS front-line missions today and in the future. The FY 2016 President's Budget will fund key priorities including a DHS data framework, enhancing information sharing between critical vetting programs; and service life extension of radiation portal monitors to sustain compliance with the SAFE Port Act. In this mission area, the FY 2016 President's Budget includes funding requests for the following key investments:

- $3.7 billion for Transportation Security Administration (TSA) screening operations to continue aviation security at prior year levels, and more effectively align passenger screening resources based on risk. These risk-based security initiatives maximize security capabilities and expedite the screening process for low-risk travelers.

- Support for U.S. Customs and Border Protection's (CBP) Trusted Traveler Programs (TTP), which provide expedited travel for pre-approved, low-risk travelers through dedicated lanes and kiosks. CBP's Trusted Traveler Programs reached record numbers of enrollment in FY 2014. An additional 1.25 million people enrolled in the agency's Trusted Traveler Programs (Global Entry, SENTRI, NEXUS and FAST) in FY 2014 to bring total enrollment to more than 3.3 million members. Global Entry, the agency's largest program with more than 1.7 million members, is operational at 42 U.S. airports and 12 Preclearance locations, serving 99 percent of incoming travelers to the United States. CBP added nine Global Entry kiosk locations this fiscal year and enrolled its one millionth member in NEXUS.

- $101 million for Radiological and Nuclear Detection Equipment Acquisition with which the Domestic Nuclear Detection Office and other DHS components, including the Coast Guard, CBP, and TSA, keep U.S. ports of entry safe and secure by detecting and interdicting illicit radioactive or nuclear materials.

- $94.5 million for Infrastructure Security Compliance funding to secure America's high-risk chemical facilities through the systematic regulation, inspection, and enforcement under the authority of the Chemical Facility Anti-Terrorism Standards. The request includes $16 million to enhance regulation of the sale and transfer of ammonium nitrate.

- $86.7 million to enhance White House Complex security, consistent with the recommendations of the United States Secret Service (USSS) Protective Missions Panel.

- $83.3 million for the BioWatch Program to provide detection and early warning of the intentional release of select aerosolized biological agents.

- $29.4 million for the Electronic Visa Information Update System (EVIUS). This new program will allow non-immigrant visa holders to provide updated biographic and travel related information through a public website. The system will complement the existing visa application process and enhance CBP's ability to make pre-travel risk determinations.

- $65.8 million for the National Protection and Programs Directorate Replacement Biometric System. This system will replace the legacy Automated Biometric Identification System. In addition to reduced operating costs, the new system will have improved detection capabilities, more efficient processing, and improved scalability.

Secure and Manage Our Borders

The Department has committed, with positive effects, historic levels of front-line personnel, technology, and infrastructure to border security to reduce the flow of illegal immigrants and illicit contraband while fostering legal trade and travel. In the future, DHS will more effectively execute its border security responsibilities by implementing a new DHS-wide, inter-component Campaign for securing the U.S. Southern Border and approaches. This Campaign will direct DHS resources in a much more collaborative fashion with pre-identified, Secretary-approved, outcomes and targets for the range of threats and challenges, including illegal migration, illegal drug, human and arms trafficking, the illicit financing of all these operations, and the terrorist threat. The FY 2016 Budget supports this effort by requesting resources needed to support officer and agent staffing along the border, maintaining all statutory personnel floors, while supporting the 2,000 additional U.S. Customs and Border Protection (CBP) officers first funded in FY 2014. The Budget retains critical border patrol, watch-list, and targeting technology that enhance the capabilities of front-line officers and agents, and investments in Coast Guard recapitalization. Funding is included for securing and managing our borders in the following key areas:

- Salaries, benefits, and operating costs for 21,370 Border Patrol agents and 23,871 CBP officers.

- Resources to complete the hiring and training of up to 2,000 new CBP officers, to achieve a total end-strength of 23,871 CBP officers. This effort, which commenced in FY 2014, is already yielding faster processing and inspection of passengers and cargo at U.S. ports of entry, as well as more seizures of illegal items, such as drugs, guns, and counterfeit goods.

- Resources for Coast Guard port security screening to secure key transportation nodes through security/background checks to ensure unauthorized and illicit individuals do not gain access to, or disrupt, key transportation and commerce nodes. All crew, passengers, and cargo of vessels over 300 tons are screened prior to arrival in U.S. waters, to mitigate potential risks to our borders.

- $373.5 million to maintain the necessary infrastructure and technology along the Nation's borders to ensure law enforcement personnel are supported with effective surveillance technology to improve their ability to detect and interdict illegal activity in a safer environment.

- Provides funds for the costs associated with apprehension and care of up to 104,000 unaccompanied children. A portion of these funds will be used to prepare facilities for families and unaccompanied children in the event of a surge that exceeds prior year apprehension levels. The request proposes up to $162 million in contingency obligation authority—enabling CBP and ICE to respond effectively in the event migration volume significantly surpasses prior-year levels.

- Support for Coast Guard recapitalization to include $340 million for production of six Fast Response Cutters; $102 million to convert Air National Guard C-27J aircraft for Coast Guard use; $91.4 million for National Security Cutter structural enhancement and post-delivery activities; and $18.5 million to complete preliminary design evaluation of the Offshore Patrol Cutter. Recapitalization will ensure Coast Guard's continued ability to enforce laws and treaties and guard the maritime domain against illegal activity and potential acts of terrorism.

- $85.3 million for the Non-Intrusive Inspection (NII) Equipment Refresh and Recapitalization program. The NII systems allow for passive radiation scanning and X-ray/gamma-ray imaging of cargo and conveyances. Large scale NII systems perform 7.2 million examinations per year at the ports of entry. In FY 2016, DHS will begin replacement of NII systems that exceed designed life expectancy.

- $89.9 million for Coast Guard operations and maintenance funds to support the delivery of new and more capable assets, including $17.2 million in operations and maintenance for two new Coast Guard Fast Response Cutters, which will provide critical maritime border security along the Atlantic and Gulf Coasts.

Enforce and Administer Our Immigration Laws

Each year Congress provides the Department resources for the prioritized removal of a portion of those living unlawfully in the United States. DHS allocates its resources to address the highest risks, targeting criminal aliens who pose a threat to public safety, recent border crossers, and employers who ignore our immigration laws. The FY 2016 Budget continues the Administration's efforts to more effectively focus the enforcement system and our finite resources on identifying and removing high-priority individuals. For FY 2016, the Budget includes funds to enable ICE to maintain more than the 34,000 detention beds and other funds requested for enforcing and administering our immigration laws, including the following:

- $3.3 billion to provide safe, secure, and humane detention and removal of removable individuals who are held in Government custody because they present a risk of flight, a risk to public safety, or are subject to mandatory detention.

    o Funds to supervise approximately 87,000 individuals (average per day by the end of FY 2016), including an additional $94.5 million to support adult detention beds for higher risk individuals and $122.5 million for the more cost-effective Alternatives to Detention program for those who are not considered a threat to our communities. The Alternatives to Detention program places low-risk individuals under various forms of intensive supervision or electronic monitoring rather than in detention.

    o $129.4 million to identify and apprehend immigration fugitives in the United States, with an emphasis on those who pose the greatest risk to national security and public safety.

    o $345.3 million to fund an increased number of family beds to address the surge in families with children crossing the U.S. southern border illegally.

    o The FY 2016 President's Budget proposes $45 million of Custody Operations funding be appropriated as five-year funding. This extension of funds availability (from one to five years) would allow ICE to improve the cost efficiency of detention bed rates.

Safeguard and Secure Cyberspace

Cybersecurity is of growing relevance to our national and economic security. Funding in this request supports the Department's two flagship cyber acquisition programs—the National Cybersecurity Protection System and Continuous Diagnostics and Mitigation—which enhance cybersecurity situational awareness and information sharing. Funding is also included to sustain the USSS network of 46 Financial Crimes Task Forces and 38 Electronic Crimes Task Forces which continues to leverage USSS partnerships with international law enforcement agencies through overseas field offices. In addition, the Department recognizes that it must maintain its own robust internal network security to be a national leader in cybersecurity. Therefore, DHS is allocating resources across all of its Components that own information technology systems as part of a plan to fix known system vulnerabilities and is preparing to implement National Protection and Programs

Directorate continuous monitoring services. The Budget includes the following key resources for safeguarding and securing cyberspace:

- The FY 2016 President's Budget sustains ICE and USSS resources to combat cyber-crime and investigate cyber-criminals.

- $479.8 million for Network Security Deployment, including the EINSTEIN3 Accelerated program which enables DHS to detect malicious traffic targeting federal (non-Department of Defense) networks and prevent malicious traffic from harming those networks.

- $102.6 million for the Continuous Diagnostics and Mitigation program which provides hardware, software, and services designed to support activities that strengthen the operational security of federal (non-Department of Defense) networks.

- $5.1 million for the CyberSkills Management Support Initiative. This initiative is intended to bolster DHS's ability to develop and maintain a robust cybersecurity workforce. As part of this initiative, DHS will ensure consistent execution of cybersecurity workforce support activities across the Department by consolidating these activities within the Office of the Chief Human Capital Officer, consistent with other workforce management programs.

Strengthen National Preparedness and Resilience

No matter the time of day or location on a map, a disaster can strike and overwhelm any of our Nation's communities. It is the goal of DHS to build a ready and resilient Nation through efforts to bolster disaster response information sharing and collaboration. The FY 2016 President's Budget supports the DRF, grant programs, disaster preparedness plans, and training for our homeland security and law enforcement partners. Working closely with State, local, and tribal governments across the country, the Federal Emergency Management Agency (FEMA) will continue to make progress in its ability to plan, prepare for, and respond to disasters.

Understanding and preparing for the impacts of a changing climate is also an Administration priority. Climate change—including an increase in prolonged periods of high temperatures, changes in precipitation, an increase in wildfires, more severe droughts, permafrost thawing, ocean acidification, and sea-level rise—is already impacting the Nation and will exacerbate many of our existing vulnerabilities. Managing these risks requires deliberate preparation, close cooperation, and coordinated planning across government, as well as by other stakeholders. The FY 2016 President's Budget includes the following climate resilience investments which will strengthen our preparedness for the effects of climate change:

- $9.6 billion to support disaster resiliency, primarily through the grants programs that are administered by FEMA and the DRF, which include:

  o $7.4 billion in DRF funding to provide immediate and long-lasting assistance to individuals and communities stricken by emergencies and major disasters.

  o $2.2 billion in total grants funding to prepare state and local governments to prevent, protect against, respond to, and recover from incidents of terrorism and other catastrophic events. These funds also include Firefighter Assistance and Emergency

Management Performance Grants that support local first responders in achieving their missions.

- $616 million in support of the President's Climate Resilience Initiatives:

  o $400 million to support flood mapping and risk analysis activities, which are essential to educating communities about flood risk and minimizing the loss of life and property as a result of flooding.

  o $200 million in Pre-Disaster Mitigation Grants for hazard mitigation planning and/or project applications to mitigate damage associated with natural disasters.

  o $10 million for analyses of climate change impacts on infrastructure critical to national and economic security, and national public health and safety.

  o $6 million for FEMA climate workshops and regional resilience coordination.

Total Budget Authority
Dollars in Thousands

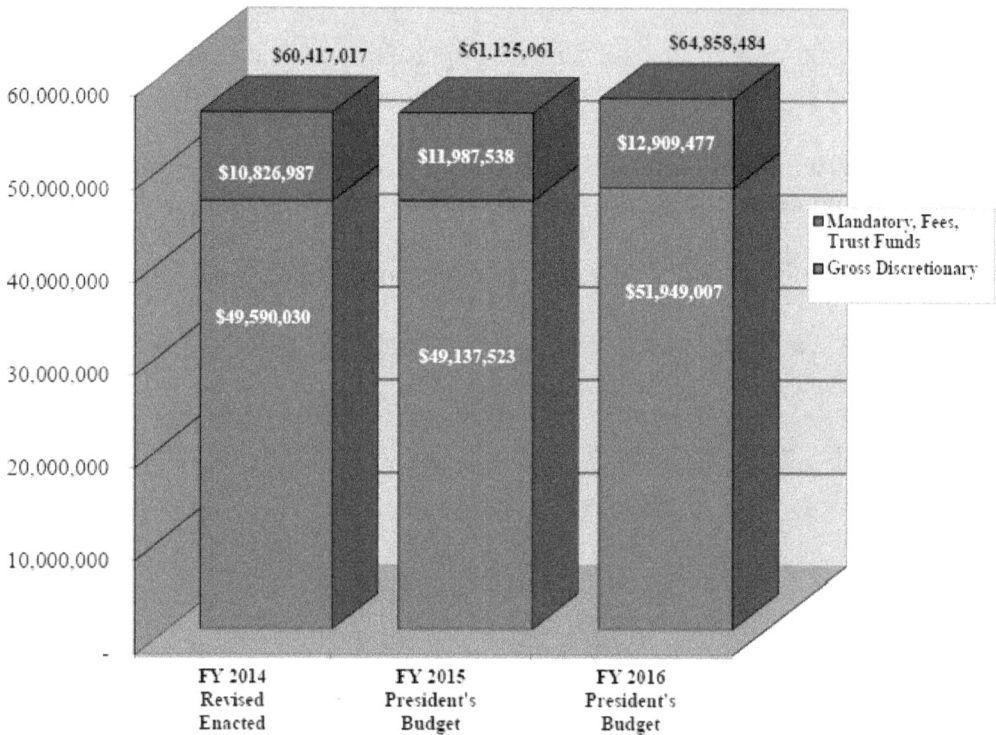

- FY 2016 Total Budget Authority funding increases by $3.7 billion, or 6.1 percent over FY 2015.

- FY 2016 estimated Mandatory Fees and Trusts budget authority increase by $922.0 million, or 7.7 percent over FY 2015.

- FY 2016 Gross Discretionary funding increases by $2.8 billion, or 5.7 percent over FY 2015.

FY 2016 Percent of Total Budget Authority by Organization
$64,858,484,000

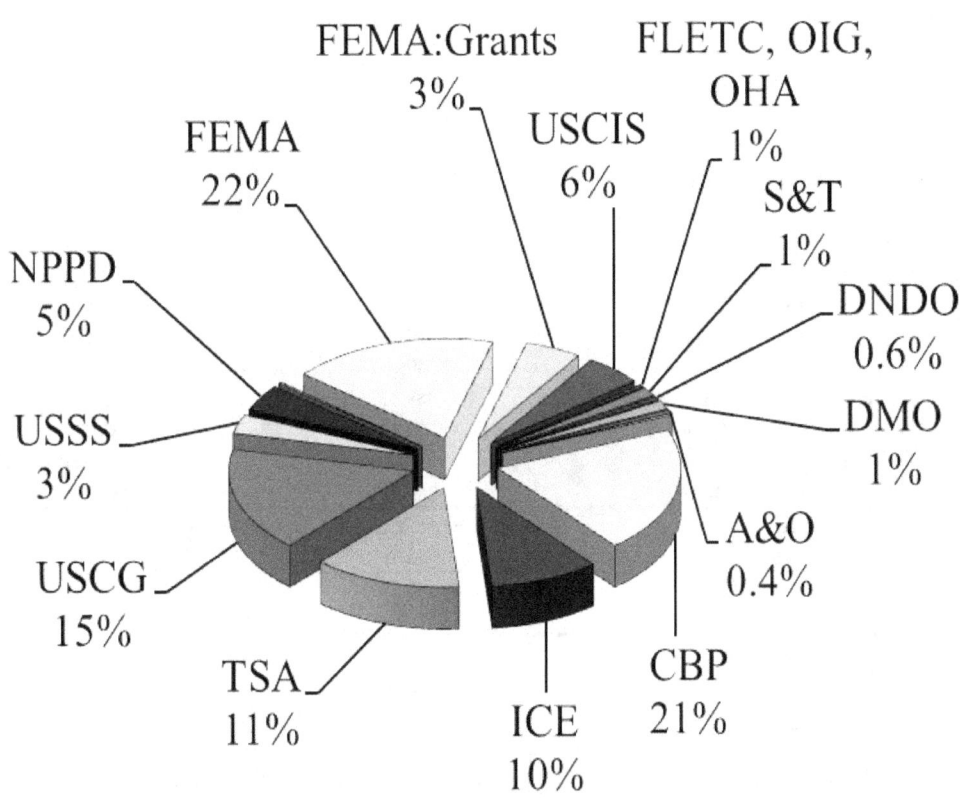

Notes:

• Departmental Management and Operations is comprised of the Office of the Secretary & Executive Management, DHS Headquarters Consolidation, the Office of the Undersecretary for Management, the Office of the Chief Financial Officer, and the Office of the Chief Information Officer

Total Budget Authority by Organization
Gross Discretionary, Mandatory, Fees, and Trust Funds

		FY 2014 Revised Enacted		FY 2015 Pres. Budget		FY 2016 Pres. Budget		FY 2016 +/- FY 2015	FY 2016 +/- FY 2015
		$000		$000		$000		$000	%
Departmental Management and Operations (DMO)	$	728,269	$	748,024	$	960,627	$	212,603	28.4%
Analysis and Operations (A&O)		300,490		302,268		269,090		(33,178)	-11.0%
Office of the Inspector General (OIG)		139,437		145,457		166,284		20,827	14.3%
U.S. Customs & Border Protection (CBP)		12,463,893		12,764,835		13,565,294		800,459	6.3%
U.S. Immigration & Customs Enforcement (ICE)		5,948,161		5,359,065		6,281,637		922,572	17.2%
Transportation Security Administration (TSA)		7,420,517		7,305,098		7,346,924		41,826	0.6%
U.S. Coast Guard (USCG)		10,098,753		9,810,468		9,963,914		153,446	1.6%
U.S. Secret Service (USSS)		1,845,272		1,895,905		2,204,122		308,217	16.3%
National Protection and Programs Directorate (NPPD)		2,810,413		2,857,666		3,102,862		245,196	8.6%
Office of Health Affairs (OHA)		126,763		125,767		124,069		(1,698)	-1.4%
Federal Emergency Management Agency (FEMA)		10,869,247		12,179,177		13,235,589		1,056,412	8.7%
FEMA: Grant Programs		2,530,000		2,225,469		2,231,424		5,955	0.3%
U.S. Citizenship & Immigration Services (USCIS)		3,368,805		3,770,026		4,003,638		233,612	6.2%
Federal Law Enforcement Training Center (FLETC)		258,730		259,595		266,694		7,099	2.7%
Science &Technology Directorate (S&T)		1,220,212		1,071,818		778,988		(292,830)	-27.3%
Domestic Nuclear Detection Office (DNDO)		288,055		304,423		357,327		52,904	17.4%
TOTAL BUDGET AUTHORITY:	$	60,417,017	$	61,125,061	$	64,858,484	$	3,733,423	6.1%
Less: Mandatory, Fee, and Trust Funds:		(10,826,987)		(11,987,538)		(12,909,477)		(921,939)	7.7%
GROSS DISC. BUDGET AUTHORITY:		49,590,030		49,137,523		51,949,007		2,811,484	5.7%
Less: Discretionary Offsetting Fees:		(3,526,605)		(4,505,990)		(4,042,340)		463,650	-10.3%
NET DISC. BUDGET AUTHORITY:	$	46,063,425	$	44,631,533	$	47,906,667	$	3,275,134	7.3%
Less: FEMA Disaster Relief - Major Disasters Cap Adjustment:	$	(5,626,386)	$	(6,437,793)	$	(6,712,953)	$	(275,160)	4.3%
Less: Rescission of Prior-Year Carryover - Regular Appropriations:		(543,968)						-	
ADJUSTED NET DISC. BUDGET AUTHORITY:	$	39,893,071	$	38,193,740	$	41,193,714	$	2,999,974	7.9%

SUMMARY INFORMATION BY DHS ORGANIZATION

DEPARTMENTAL MANAGEMENT AND OPERATIONS

Description:

Departmental Management and Operations (DMO) provides leadership, direction, and management to the Department of Homeland Security (DHS) and comprises five separate appropriations including: the Office of the Secretary and Executive Management (OSEM); the Under Secretary for Management and Management Directorate (USM); the Office of the Chief Financial Officer (OCFO); the Office of the Chief Information Officer (OCIO); and DHS Headquarters (HQ) Consolidation.

OSEM includes the Immediate Office of the Secretary and Deputy Secretary; Office of the Chief of Staff; Office of the Executive Secretary; Office of Intergovernmental Affairs (IGA); Office of Policy; Office of Public Affairs (OPA); Office of Legislative Affairs (OLA); Office of the General Counsel (OGC); Office for Civil Rights and Civil Liberties (CRCL); Privacy Office (PRIV); and Office of the Citizenship and Immigration Services Ombudsman.

USM includes the Immediate Office of the Under Secretary for Management, Office of the Chief Human Capital Officer (OCHCO), Office of the Chief Procurement Officer (OCPO), Office of the Chief Readiness Support Officer (CRSO), and Office of the Chief Security Officer.

OCFO comprises the Budget Division, Program Analysis and Evaluation Division, Financial Operations Division, Office of Financial Management, Risk Management and Assurance Division, Resource Management Transformation Office, Financial Assistance Policy & Oversight Division, Departmental General Accountability Office/Office of Inspector General Audit Liaison Office, Cost Analysis Division, and Workforce Development Division.

OCIO comprises the Information Security Office, Information Sharing Environment Office, Enterprise Business Management Office, Enterprise Systems Development Office, Geospatial Information Office, Office of Accessible Systems and Technology, and the Information Technology Services Office.

Responsibilities:

OSEM provides central leadership, management, direction, and oversight over all of the Department's Components.

USM is responsible for Department-wide mission support services and oversight for all DMO functions, including: information technology (IT), budget and financial management, procurement and acquisition, human capital, security, logistics and facilities, and oversight of the Working

__At a Glance__

Senior Leadership:
Jeh Johnson, Secretary
Alejandro Mayorkas, Deputy Secretary
Chip Fulghum, Chief Financial Officer
Luke McCormack, Chief Information Officer

Established: 2003 under the Department of Homeland Security Act of 2002

Major Divisions: Office of the Secretary and Executive Management; Office of the Under Secretary for Management; Office of the Chief Readiness Support Officer; Office of Chief Human Capital Officer; Office of the Chief Procurement Officer; Office of the Chief Security Officer; Office of the Chief Financial Officer; Office of the Chief Information Officer

Budget Request: $960,627,000

Employees (FTE): 2,029

Capital Fund (WCF) service delivery. The USM provides the overarching management structure for the Department to deliver customer service, while eliminating redundancies and reducing support costs in order to more effectively and efficiently run the Department in a unified manner.

OCFO is responsible for the fiscal management, integrity, and accountability of DHS. The mission of OCFO is to provide guidance and oversight of the Department's budget and financial management, and oversee financial operations for DMO. OCFO also manages the DHS WCF, grants and assistance awards, and resource management systems to ensure that funds necessary to carry out the Department's mission are obtained, allocated, and efficiently expended in accordance with the Department's priorities and relevant law and policies.

OCIO is responsible for the IT projects of the Department. OCIO provides IT leadership, IT governance, products, and services to ensure the effective and appropriate use of IT across DHS. OCIO coordinates acquisition strategies to minimize costs and improve consistency of the infrastructure, and enhances mission success by partnering with other DHS Components to leverage the best available information technologies and management practices. OCIO is the lead office in providing the capability for DHS to partner in the sharing of essential information to Federal, State, local, and tribal governments, and private industry. OCIO also leads the DHS Information Security Program, which includes oversight and coordination of activities associated with the Federal Information Security Management Act.

The DHS HQ Consolidation Project is focused on the co-location and consolidation of the Department through lease consolidation and coordination of the St. Elizabeths campus development with the General Services Administration. Continuing prudent consolidation efforts enhances the ability of the Department to carry out its mission sets in the most effective and efficient way possible.

Service to the Public:

The Secretary ensures a coordinated effort to build a safe, secure, and resilient homeland by directing the Department's efforts to prevent terrorism and enhance security, secure and manage our borders, enforce and administer our Nation's immigration laws, safeguard and secure cyberspace, ensure resilience to disasters, and support national and economic security.

FY 2014 Accomplishments:

- The Secretary established the Joint Requirements Council to integrate the mission requirements of the operational Components, resulting in recommendations for investment, training, organization, legislation, and operational processes and procedures. This work will inform the Department's program and budget review and acquisition review process, and will enhance operational effectiveness.

- The Office of the General Counsel provided legal support and cross-Component coordination for the Department's response to the influx of unaccompanied children at the southwest border and for the Department's response to Ebola outbreak.

- The Office of Public Affairs and the U.S. Citizenship and Immigration Services (CIS) Ombudsman continued public outreach in support of the "If You See Something, Say Something™" campaign and the "Blue Campaign."

- CRCL Community Engagement coordinated and participated in more than 100 engagement events in 2014, encompassing approximately 60 standing roundtables held in 14 cities across the country, 26 secondary meetings and events associated with standing roundtables, and 14 individual engagement events. CRCL is currently active in 16 metropolitan areas with 14 regularly held roundtable meetings.

- The Office of Legislative Affairs managed, oversaw, and provided support to 180 DHS witnesses testifying at 123 hearings before multiple congressional committees and subcommittees.

- The Privacy Office spearheaded a briefing of the DHS Data Framework Project, which is a scalable IT program with built-in capabilities to support advanced data architecture and governance processes, for the White House's Big Data and Privacy Study, "Big Data: Seizing Opportunities, Preserving Value." PRIV also contributed significantly to a chapter on the DHS Data Framework in the broader context of embedding privacy protections in government use of big data and published four Privacy Impact Assessments related to how DHS protects privacy in the DHS Data Framework.

- The CIS Ombudsman resolved 6,135 requests for case assistance during the 2014 reporting period (a one-third increase from the prior year), of which approximately 15 percent were related to the Deferred Action for Childhood Arrivals program.

- The Policy Office released the 2014 Quadrennial Homeland Security Review, which reflects deep analysis of the evolving strategic environment, outlines the specific strategic priorities necessary to keep the Nation secure, and serves as an important foundational step to advance the Secretary's Departmental Unity of Effort priority.

- The Office of Intergovernmental Affairs, as the Department's lead for the Council of Governors, led the development of a signed Cyber Joint Action Plan that is currently being implemented by DHS, the Department of Defense and all 50 States via the National Governors Association; additionally, during the influx of unaccompanied children along the southwest border, IGA deployed four individuals to Texas and Arizona to coordinate outreach to State and local elected and appointed officials to ensure consistent communication and immediate access to accurate information on this evolving issue.

- The Chief Financial Officer (CFO) made enhancements to strengthen the Department's programming and budgeting process. During development of the FYs 2016–2020 budget, CFO further focused on the way DHS invests its resources across Components to better support primary mission areas. CFO further supported the Secretary's Unity of Effort initiative by incorporating the results of enhanced departmental joint requirements planning and strategic analysis efforts into the budget process. By improving the budget process, the Department is now better able to ensure resources support key priorities, and more accurately project the impact of budget decisions on the Department's critical resources, including staffing, capital acquisitions, and operations, among others.

- The CFO led the effort to maintain the clean opinion this year in addition to continuing to reduce material weaknesses in internal controls.

- The Chief Human Capital Officer achieved the President's Council on Veterans Employment FY 2014 hiring goals; in FY 2014, new hires who are veterans were the highest percentage on record at 27.6% for veterans and 9.6% for veterans with disabilities. The Department maintains the goal of employing 50,000 veterans across the Department.

- The Chief Procurement Office was awarded 10 new Strategic Sourcing initiatives, including Detection Equipment, Language Services, and additional Enterprise License Agreements.

- The Chief Procurement Office received an "A" grade from the U.S. Small Business Administration for exceeding goals for the procurement of goods and services from small, disadvantaged, and veteran-owned businesses.

- The Chief Information Officer surpassed the FY 2014 Identity, Credential, and Access Management–Office of Management and Budget goal of 75 percent, with 81 percent of users now on strong authentication (i.e., Homeland Security Presidential Directive (HSPD) -12 Logical Access) on sensitive but unclassified networks.

- The Chief Information Officer successfully deployed Neptune and Common Entity Index Pilots as part of DHS Data Framework.

- The Chief Information Officer established an environment where 50 reusable services were deployed in the DHS Private Cloud, allowing access to information and pre-built applications in a central repository enabling more efficient migration of the Department's Component Web sites such as ICE.gov and FLETC.gov.

- CRSO established the DHS Aviation Governance Board with CRSO designated as the chair to develop plans and initiatives to improve integration of U.S. Customs and Border Protection, United States Coast Guard, and U.S. Immigration and Customs Enforcement aviation mission support.

- The Chief Security Office completed the Lenel Disaster Recovery system upgrade, which improved standardization, reliability, and customer use of the Physical Access Control System.

BUDGET REQUEST

Dollars in Thousands

	FY 2014 Revised Enacted		FY 2015 President's Budget		FY 2016 President's Budget		FY 2016 +/- FY 2015	
	FTE	$000	FTE	$000	FTE	$000	FTE	$000
Office of the Secretary and Executive Management	563	$122,350	583	$128,769	597	$134,247	14	$5,478
Office of the Under Secretary for Management	872	196,015	854	195,286	822	193,187	(32)	(2,099)
DHS HQ Consolidation	0	35,000	0	73,000	0	215,822	0	142,822
Office of the Chief Financial Officer	208	75,548	212	94,626	228	96,775	16	2,149
Office of the Chief Information Officer	274	299,356	290	256,343	382	320,596	92	64,253
Net Discretionary	**1,917**	**$728,269**	**1,939**	**$748,024**	**2,029**	**$960,627**	**90**	**$212,603**
Total Budget Authority	**1,917**	**$728,269**	**1,939**	**$748,024**	**2,029**	**$960,627**	**90**	**$212,603**
Less prior year Rescissions	0	(209)	0	0	0	0	0	0
Total	**1,971**	**$728,060**	**1,939**	**$748,024**	**2,029**	**$960,627**	**90**	**$212,603**

FY 2016 Highlights:

- **Joint Requirements Council (JRC)**..$5.0M (3 FTE)
  The JRC will formulate recommendations to DHS leadership on options to meet the capability needs of DHS operators and provide a vital link between strategic guidance and investments.

- **HQ Consolidation**.. $204.3M (0 FTE)
  The funding will support the development of the Center Building addition, relocation of the Management Directorate in entirety to St. Elizabeths, build-out of the remaining DHS Operations Center (DOC) A, the Employee Assistance Center/Health Unit, and Munro Building reconfiguration which will increase utilization.

- **Financial Systems Modernization**...$43.0M (0 FTE)
  This funding will support requirements related to Component migrations to new financial systems. Various DHS Components are seeking to transition to a financial management solution that eliminates operational constraints, fills existing mission gaps, complies with Federal requirements and guidelines, and provides a fully automated, integrated, streamlined, and reliable core financial system.

- **Single Sign-On** .... $16.2M (1 FTE)
  Single Sign-on for DHS aims to reduce the number of times an employee needs to logon to one system. This initiative will improve the cyber security posture of the Department and reduce lost productivity time, operational costs, and help desk calls.

- **Digital Services Team**.. **$10.0M (38 FTE)**
  The DHS Digital Services team will be responsible for driving the efficiency and
  effectiveness of the Department's highest-impact digital services with the DHS Chief
  Information Officer serving as the senior accountable official. The DHS Digital Services
  team is designed to build and implement software products used by citizens, businesses, and
  government employees to execute the Department's core missions.

- **DHS Data Framework** .... **$7.1M (4 FTE)**
  The combination of the Neptune, Common Entity Index, and Cerberus projects under the
  Controlled Homeland Information Sharing Environment strategy and Data Framework will
  effectively safeguard data, and provide the Department with the ability to increase
  productivity of analysts, reduce the information-sharing burden, expand the capacity of
  mission-driven decision-making analysis, and improve the integrity of mission-critical
  information.

- **CyberSkills Management Support Initiative (CMSI)**................................ **$5.1M (7 FTE)**
  CMSI will be able to reach and collaborate with Component senior and human capital
  leadership to ensure consistent adoption of and support for cybersecurity workforce support
  activities. Department-wide human capital strategies, policies, and programs to enhance the
  DHS cybersecurity workforce would be created and managed from the same organization
  focused on similar initiatives for the entire DHS workforce.

FY 2016 Major Decreases:
- **OneNet**.. **-$1.8M (0 FTE)**
  The Infrastructure Transformation Program represents the Department's full-scale move
  toward a DHS-consolidated IT infrastructure supporting the cross-organizational missions of
  protecting the homeland, deterring crime, detecting and countering threats, and myriad other
  responsibilities. Although the proposed reduction will affect OneNet, every effort will be
  made to use remaining resources efficiently to maintain a robust program.

ANALYSIS AND OPERATIONS

Description:

The Analysis and Operations appropriation provides resources for the support of the Office of Intelligence and Analysis (I&A) and the Office of Operations Coordination (OPS). This appropriation includes both National Intelligence Program (NIP) and non-NIP funds for I&A and non-NIP funds for OPS.

Responsibilities:

The Analysis and Operations appropriation provides resources for the support of I&A and OPS. While these two offices are distinct in their missions, they work closely together and collaborate with other DHS Components and Federal agencies, as well as State, local, tribal, territorial (SLTT), foreign, and private-sector partners to improve intelligence analysis, information sharing, incident management support, and situational awareness.

> *At a Glance*
>
> *Senior Leadership:*
> *Francis X. Taylor*
> *Under Secretary of Intelligence and Analysis*
>
> *Richard Chavez,*
> *Director, Office of Operations Coordination*
>
> *Established: 2006*
>
> *Major Divisions: Office of Intelligence and Analysis; Office of Operations Coordination*
>
> ***Budget Request: $269,090,000***
>
> *Employees (FTE): 834*

I&A's mission is to equip the homeland security enterprise (HSE) with the intelligence and information it needs to keep the Homeland safe, secure, and resilient. I&A has a unique role as a central conduit for information sharing among the Intelligence Community (IC); federal entities; SLTT entities through the National Network of Fusion Centers (NNFC); and nontraditional partners to support the goals of the Quadrennial Homeland Security Review. This includes promoting an understanding of threats to the Homeland through intelligence analysis, coordinating the counterintelligence activities of the Department, collecting information and intelligence to support homeland security missions, managing intelligence for the HSE, and sharing the information necessary for action while protecting the privacy, civil rights, and civil liberties of all Americans. OPS operates across the five incident and crisis management mission areas (prevent, protect, mitigate, respond, recover) and enables unity of effort throughout the homeland security enterprise. OPS has unique statutory and regulatory roles and responsibilities as the focal point for information sharing, decision support products, situational awareness and coordination among the DHS, Federal, SLTT, non-governmental, and international operations and fusion centers. OPS executes these roles and responsibilities utilizing multiple incident and crisis management mechanisms. Additionally, OPS ensures the resilience of DHS's overall mission through its leadership of the Department's Continuity of Operations Program.

Service to the Public:

Analysis and Operations resources enable the critical support necessary to the homeland security mission by improving the analysis and sharing of threat information. This includes advising all levels of government (federal and SLTT), the private sector, and the public with timely information concerning threats to the Homeland.

I&A analyzes intelligence and information about homeland security threats and serves as the two-way interface between the IC, SLTT, and private sector partners on homeland security intelligence and information. This includes warnings, actionable intelligence, and analysis to ensure that Headquarters leadership, departmental operating Components, federal policymakers, federal law enforcement and IC partners, and frontline law enforcement have the information they need to confront and disrupt terrorist and other threats to the Homeland. I&A has a unique analytic mission, blending intelligence from the IC with DHS Component, SLTT, and other stakeholder source data, to provide homeland security-centric intelligence products to federal, SLTT, and private sector decision makers. The Under Secretary for Intelligence and Analysis leads I&A and is the Department's Chief Intelligence Officer, responsible for managing the entire DHS Intelligence Enterprise (IE). The Under Secretary is also the Department's Information Sharing and Safeguarding Executive responsible for facilitating information sharing, implementing the objectives of the Department and the National Strategy on Information Sharing within DHS while ensuring that such information is protected from unauthorized disclosure. Additionally, the Under Secretary serves as the DHS Counterintelligence Executive, leading the DHS Counterintelligence Program in its efforts to protect departmental personnel and information against foreign intelligence activities.

OPS provides information and decision support products before, during and after a threat or disaster. The information and support tools are provided 24 hours a day, seven days a week, to assist senior officials at all levels of government and private sector in preventing, protecting, mitigating, responding to, and recovering from threats and disasters. OPS collects, analyzes and disseminates all-threats and all-hazards information from a wide variety of sources to include Federal, State, local, tribal, territorial, and international governments, as well as the private sector and traditional and social media sources.

OPS, in coordination with other DHS Components and Federal, SLTT, private sector, and international partners works to integrate incident and crisis management activities across the DHS mission areas. OPS manages the National Operations Center (NOC), the Secretary's Briefing Staff (SBS), and the Department's Special Events Program, providing situational awareness, administrative and operations support for a wide range of homeland security activities, threats, incidents, and events each year. Additionally, the Director of OPS serves as the DHS Continuity Coordinator, ensuring the resilience of all DHS Primary Mission Essential Functions (PMEFs) and Mission Essential Functions in the event of a disaster, and maintains emergency preparedness within the Department.

2014 Accomplishments:

I&A

- I&A supported and monitored capability that strengthened the four Critical Operational Capabilities (COCs): receive, analyze, disseminate, and gather — and the four Enabling Capabilities (ECs): privacy, civil rights and civil liberties protections; sustainment strategy, communications and outreach; and security. Over the last three fiscal years, the annual NNFC assessment score has moved from 76.8 percent to almost 92 percent; results that the Office of the Director of Intelligence recognizes as demonstrative of the success of I&A's support to the NNFC.

- I&A—in close cooperation with the Kentucky Intelligence Fusion Center (KIFC) and other partners—briefed over 120 private-sector and SLTT partners in Lexington, Kentucky, on active shooter and cyber threats, as well as response and mitigation strategies, as part of I&A's regional Corporate Security Symposium Program. Hosted by the Louisville Gas and Electric/Kentucky Utilities, this event featured analysts from Walmart, Target, DHS (I&A, National Protection and Programs Directorate (NPPD), and U.S. Secret Service), FBI, and the KIFC. The Symposium prompted discussion on actions private sector and SLTT entities can take to mitigate cyber and active shooter threats, and Federal and State government resources available to them. This event, the first FY 2014 Corporate security Symposium, provided a forum for public and private-sector partners to collaborate and establish relationships.

- I&A kept Department leadership and staff informed of the threat from foreign intelligence organizations, primarily focusing on cyber and supply chain threats. The targeted analysis enabled DHS security personnel to better mitigate potential threats to Department personnel and information.

- I&A provided over 300 threat briefings for State, local, tribal, territorial, and private-sector partners, enabling the partners to improve security capabilities, adapt security postures, and increase operational awareness and planning related to their efforts to deter, prevent, preempt, or respond to terrorist attacks against the United States.

- I&A managed the Watch-listing Training and Certification Program, expanding by almost 400 percent the pool of DHS watch-listing analysts and ensuring Department information is properly reflected in national terrorist databases.

OPS

- OPS monitored over 19,000 items of interest ranging from suspicious activity to natural disasters and shared information with homeland security partners.

- OPS managed 1,193 executive communications from senior leadership and convened 1,903 teleconferences with both intra- and interagency partners.

- OPS vetted over 3,700 Known or Suspected Terrorists (KSTs); enhanced over 2,100 Terrorism Identities DataMart Environment (TIDE) records; and watch-listed more than 200 sets of KSTs' fingerprints in the Automated Fingerprint Identification System (IDENT).

- OPS vetted more than 15,000 immigration cases; identified more than 800 naturalization fraud cases and 1,600 immigration benefit fraud cases; created lookouts in the Treasury Enforcement Communication System (TECS); and facilitated 174 visa and/or travel authorization revocations as well as 360 field enforcement encounters.

- OPS ensured DHS met 100 percent of 2014 Eagle Horizon reporting requirements over a 45-day period. This effort involved 11 components, 900 personnel, and 13 continuity sites.

- OPS conducted a comprehensive revalidation and verification of Mission Essential Functions with all DHS components, and identified 10 Primary Mission Essential Functions, which were referred to the Secretary and the White House Independent Review Board.

- OPS expanded the use of the DHS Common Operating Picture (DHS COP) and Request for Information (RFI) tools to Federal operations centers, State and major urban area fusion and emergency operations centers to support emergency and incident management.

- OPS deployed DHS Common Operating Picture (DHS COP) Mobile and expanded the DHS COP user base to over 34,000 users while removing the dependency on accessing the DHS COP from a government-issued workstation.

- Homeland Security Information Network (HSIN) launched a Multi-State Facial Recognition Community making it possible for vetted users to initiate facial recognition requests to all 18 current participating states and fusion centers with a single click of the mouse.

- OPS supported two National Special Security Events (NSSEs) and 17 Special Event Assessment Rating (SEAR) events.

- OPS conducted 19 National Planner's courses as well as deployed six mobile training teams, training 495 planners throughout the homeland security enterprise.

BUDGET REQUEST
Dollars in Thousands

	FY 2014 Revised Enacted		FY 2015 President's Budget		FY 2016 President's Budget		FY 2016 +/- FY 2015	
	FTE	$000	FTE	$000	FTE	$000	FTE	$000
Analysis and Operations	845	$300,490	850	$302,268	834	$269,090	(16)	($33,178)
Automation Modernization	-	-						
Construction	-	-						
Net Discretionary	**845**	**$300,490**	**850**	**$302,268**	**834**	**$269,090**	**(16)**	**($33,178)**
Offsetting Collections		-						
Gross Discretionary	**845**	**$300,490**	**850**	**$302,268**	**834**	**$269,090**	**(16)**	**($33,178)**
Mandatory/Fees	-	-						
Total Budget Authority	**845**	**$300,490**	**850**	**$302,268**	**834**	**$269,090**	**(16)**	**($33,178)**
Less prior year Rescissions	-	($375)						
Total	**845**	**$300,115**	**850**	**$302,268**	**834**	**$269,090**	**(16)**	**($33,178)**

FY 2016 Highlights:

Funding and personnel for Analysis and Operations highlights are classified.

OFFICE OF THE INSPECTOR GENERAL

Description:

The Department of Homeland Security (DHS) Office of Inspector General (OIG) was established by the *Homeland Security Act of 2002* (P.L. 107-296) by an amendment to the *Inspector General Act of 1978*. The OIG has a dual reporting responsibility to the Secretary of DHS and to the Congress. The OIG serves as an independent and objective audit, inspection, and investigative body to promote economy, effectiveness, and efficiency in DHS programs and operations, and to prevent and detect fraud, waste, and abuse in these programs and operations.

At a Glance

Senior Leadership: John Roth, Inspector General

Established: 2003

Major Divisions: Audits, Emergency Management Oversight, Information Technology Audits, Inspections, Integrity and Quality Oversight, and Investigations

Budget Request: $166,284,000

Employees (FTE): 796

Responsibilities:

The OIG conducts and supervises audits, inspections, special reviews, and investigations of the Department's programs and operations. The OIG examines, evaluates and, where necessary, critiques these operations and activities, recommending ways for DHS to carry out its responsibilities in the most economical, efficient, and effective manner possible. The OIG reviews recommendations regarding existing and proposed legislation and regulations relating to the Department's programs and operations.

In addition, the OIG is responsible for the oversight of all DHS contracts, grants, and governmental operations related to ongoing disaster relief operations and counterterrorism efforts. The OIG ensures that this oversight encompasses an aggressive and ongoing audit and investigative effort designed to identify and address fraud, waste, and abuse. The OIG also coordinates the audit activities of other Inspectors General who oversee funds transferred to their respective departments and agencies by the Federal Emergency Management Agency (FEMA).

The OIG operates a web-based and call center Hotline, as a resource for Federal employees and the public to report allegations of employee corruption, civil rights and civil liberties abuses, program fraud and financial crimes, and miscellaneous criminal and non-criminal activity associated with waste, abuse, or fraud affecting the programs and operations of the Department. The Hotline provides confidentiality and anonymity for callers who may be whistleblowers.

Service to the Public:

The OIG safeguards the public's tax dollars by preventing and detecting fraud, waste, and abuse in the Department's programs and operations and recommending more efficient and effective ways of doing business. The OIG maintains and publicizes both a web-based and toll-free hotline, which provides a prompt, effective channel for DHS employees, contract personnel, and private citizens to report incidents of fraud, waste, and abuse.

FY 2014 Accomplishments:

In Fiscal Year (FY) 2014, the OIG improved the Department's economy, efficiency, and effectiveness through audits and investigations of departmental activities, including both DHS-wide and Component programs.

During FY 2014, the OIG efforts resulted in the following accomplishments:

- Identified monetary recoveries of $72.9 million from cost disallowances and investigative activities; questionable spending of $148.1 million; and potential cost avoidance of $907.4 million if funds are put to better use.

- Investigated cases that led to 142 arrests, 87 indictments, 112 convictions, and 36 personnel actions. Fines, restitution, and administrative cost avoidance totaled $13 million.

- Closed 760 investigations, initiated 564 new investigations, and issued 695 Reports of Investigation.

- Identified areas of improvement and provided 581 recommendations to the Department's management to improve the economy, effectiveness, and efficiency of its programs.

- DHS management concurred with 98 percent of OIG's management recommendations and 96 percent of OIG's disaster grant recommendations.

To aid the Department in combating and countering terrorism, DHS OIG issued a joint report with three other Offices of Inspector General that focused attention on improving information sharing and handling of intelligence and law enforcement information to prevent events such as the Boston Marathon bombings.

With respect to cyber security and other threats, OIG audits determined that DHS has had significant challenges in complying with Federal computer security requirements, and made recommendations for improvement. OIG also issued reports addressing the Department's preparation for pandemics, the effectiveness of its Visa Security Program, and the Domestic Nuclear Detection Office's security posture against the risks posed by trusted insiders.

OIG conducted work to enhance border security and immigration enforcement, including audits of U.S. Customs and Border Protection's (CBP's) Office of Field Operations' Workload Staffing Model to determine its reliability in establishing the number of CBP Officers needed to fulfill mission requirements. OIG also conducted a series of reviews focused on CBP's efforts to handle the influx of unaccompanied children crossing the Southern border. Unlike traditional reports, OIG issued these in real time, ensuring Department leadership, Congress, and the public of immediate, meaningful oversight and enabling the Department to take timely corrective action.

OIG continued to oversee the mandatory, external, independent audit of the Department's financial statements and internal control over financial reporting. The Department continued to improve financial management in FY 2014, and achieved an unmodified (clean) opinion on all financial statements. OIG assessed that more work is needed to eliminate material weaknesses in internal control over financial reporting.

In 2014, OIG issued 14 proactive disaster grant audit reports and initiated five additional audits of Hurricane Sandy relief efforts. Recognizing that the potential for fraud always exists, OIG investigators developed a robust partnership with the Recovery Accountability and Transparency Board (RATB), to leverage information technology resources and analysts to detect and remediate waste, fraud and abuse associated with Hurricane Sandy disaster relief funds. RATB is staffed, in part, by a DHS OIG investigator and an inspector on loan to the Board. The OIG submitted 48 requests to RATB for analysis, including 17 requests to support criminal investigations and 31 for audits. RATB completed 30 of the requests, which resulted in 583 new investigative leads.

BUDGET REQUEST
Dollars in Thousands

	FY 2014 Revised Enacted		FY 2015 President's Budget		FY 2016 President's Budget		FY 2016 +/- FY 2015	
	FTE	$000	FTE	$000	FTE	$000	FTE	$000
Salaries and Expenses	681	$139,437	725	$145,457	796	$166,284	71	$20,827
Gross Discretionary	681	$139,437	725	$145,457	796	$166,284	71	$20,827
Total Budget Authority	**681**	**$139,437**	**725**	**$145,457**	**796**	**$166,284**	**71**	**$20,827**
Less prior year Rescissions	-	(48)	-	-	-	-	-	-
Total	**681**	**$139,389**	**725**	**$145,457**	**796**	**$166,284**	**71**	**$20,827**

Footnote: The FY 2015 and FY 2016 President's Budget includes a $24 million transfer from FEMA Disaster Relief Fund.

FY 2016 Highlights:

- **Acquisition Management Oversight...$7.6M (40 FTE)**
  The budget provides a $7.6 million increase in FY 2016 for the Acquisition Management Oversight initiative.

  DHS has the third largest acquisition budget in the Federal Government and acquires more than $25 billion worth of goods and services annually. Current and prior OIG and Government Accountability Office reviews demonstrate that billions of taxpayer dollars and the nation's security are vulnerable to waste. Accordingly, we have designated acquisitions management as a major management challenge and a high-risk area for the Department. This initiative will allow OIG to add resources to auditing DHS' acquisition program, as well as to develop an acquisition life-cycle audit program. Instead of waiting until projects are complete, we will be able to audit projects as they develop to identify problem areas before money is spent. Increased audit coverage will help DHS improve its major acquisition programs and better control costs, meet deployment plans, and deliver capability consistent with program requirements.

- **Fraud and Computer Forensics...$6.1M (13 FTE)**
  The budget provides a $6.1 million increase in FY 2016 for the Fraud and Computer Forensics initiative to establish two related programs.

The OIG will establish a new specialized investigative unit, the Acquisition Corruption and Fraud Division (ACFD). The program increase for investigative services will support new agents, analysts, and collaborative support positions from across the OIG to handle expected increased investigative referrals from the Acquisition Management Oversight initiative. The ACFD will employ advanced analytical technology to facilitate a multitude of fraud detection and prevention training courses for DHS acquisition professionals, support acquisition-related investigations, and identify potential areas of risk for new audits and inspections.

OIG will also establish the Cyber Forensics and Analysis Division (CFAD) to provide in-house computer/digital forensics support in order to maintain investigative independence, data integrity, and the ability to provide accurate and timely analysis in furtherance of OIG's investigations, audits and inspections. The CFAD will consist of a central cyber forensics laboratory sufficiently robust to process high priority OIG investigations, audits, and inspections, develop policy and maintain future capability for equipment test and evaluation protocols.

- **Inspections and Special Reviews..…..$2.8M (14 FTE)**
  The budget provides a $2.8 million increase in FY 2016 for the Inspection and Special Reviews initiative to enable the OIG to be more responsive to congressional requests as well as to perform risk-based planning to address critical areas susceptible to waste, fraud, and abuse.

  An increase in priority requests and mandates from Congress requires more than 50 percent of the efforts of the Office of Inspections (ISP). These priority assignments have reduced OIG's ability to provide adequate coverage of other high-risk areas, including the Department's intelligence programs and issues regarding civil rights and civil liberties. Additional resources will allow OIG to initiate reviews and follow up on deficiencies identified during field work of other areas. Additional funding will provide inspectors with enhanced technology and other tools, such as contract subject matter expertise, that will increase the efficiency and effectiveness of reviews. The increase in resources will allow ISP to more timely respond to the growing requests from Congress, DHS leadership, and non-governmental organizations, without sacrificing reviews in other critical areas.

- **Cybersecurity Implementation of Continuous Monitoring ....$1.2M (3 FTE)**
  The budget provides $1.2 million increase in FY 2016 for the Cybersecurity Implementation of Continuous Monitoring initiative, which will enable the OIG to comply with the *Federal Information Security Management Act* (FISMA) as well as assessing DHS operational and cybersecurity programs for compliance with FISMA by conducting technical tests of various IT systems and assets.

  The OIG is responsible for protecting the integrity of its own network and its sensitive audit and law enforcement data, as well as ensuring the security of the portal it presents to the larger DHS network. The OIG has been participating in the DHS Federal Network Resiliency Continuous Diagnostics and Mitigation Program since its inception. This DHS program seeks to provide other Federal agencies with the tools necessary for a proper Information Security Continuous Monitoring (ISCM) Program. These ISCM tools will enable agencies to transition from a paper-based to a dashboard-based authorization cycle.

In order to leverage these ISCM tools and properly gauge risk, the OIG requires resources to oversee its ISCM Program, mitigate newly-discovered vulnerabilities, and meet the near real-time expectations of the future FISMA metrics.

Additionally, the OIG has an annual requirement to assess DHS operational and cyber security programs for compliance with the law. Part of this assessment includes technical testing of various IT systems and assets. The discovery and assessment process requires applications that scan, identify, and rate the severity of cyber vulnerabilities, which in conjunction with visual inspections and interviews of critical personnel, allows the OIG to assign a level of risk to each finding. To accomplish these requirements the OIG cybersecurity auditors must have the latest technology, both hardware and software, at their disposal to efficiently and effectively assess the security posture of DHS components.

- **Whistleblower Protection...$0.275M (1 FTE)**
  The budget provides $0.275 million to ensure DHS compliance with Title 10 U.S.C. § 1034, *Military Whistleblower Protection Act*.

  Section 1034 requires DHS OIG to investigate reprisals against members of the U.S. Coast Guard (USCG). USCG has over 41,000 active duty members and nearly 7,000 reservists stationed around the world. The law requires the Inspector General to submit a report on the results of the investigation to the Secretary of DHS and the Commandant of the Coast Guard.

  The additional investigative staff will allow the OIG to dedicate and train individuals with the necessary skill set to understand the *Military Whistleblower Protection Act*, the rights of the whistleblower, and the intricacies of how the USCG works and how its senior management functions.

- **General Services Administration (GSA) Space Build Out...................$3.1M (0 FTE)**
  The budget provides $3.1 million for the GSA Space Build Out, which will allow the OIG to reduce space by 12 percent in FY 2016.

  The FY 2016 program increase of $3.1 million supports office consolidation and relocation expenses. The one-time program increase of $3.1 million will fund build out costs to relocate OIG headquarters and will be allocated to tenant improvements, moving services, physical security, and other contingencies. Using GSA's Furniture and Information Technology Initiative, OIG will be able to absorb furniture and information technology costs necessary to relocate by adding these costs to annual GSA rent. In addition to reducing space costs, relocating to open, collaborative space will reduce OIG's carbon footprint by decreasing the amount of space required per person; and enhance the OIG's ability to respond effectively to changes in the size of its workforce without negatively impacting employee collaboration and productivity, or organizational performance.

U.S. CUSTOMS AND BORDER PROTECTION

Description:

U.S. Customs and Border Protection (CBP) is responsible for securing America's borders to protect the United States against terrorist threats and prevent the illegal entry of inadmissible persons and contraband, while facilitating lawful travel, trade, and immigration. CBP performs these missions with vigilance, integrity, and professionalism.

Responsibilities:

CBP plays an important role in the whole-of-government approach in protecting our homeland. In this role, CBP must be a national leader in developing a well-informed, agile, and seamless global network to

strengthen our border security operations, without unduly affecting the legal movement of people and goods. This network must constantly enhance and evolve its capabilities to serve common interests in combating terrorism; supporting and promoting economic growth; defining, prioritizing, and disrupting transnational criminal organizations; and preventing the spread of agricultural pests and diseases. CBP is also part of a broader public-private collaboration that extends the "zone of security" to transcend our physical borders, ensuring that the U.S. physical border is the last line of defense, not the first.

Along the over 5,000 miles of border with Canada, 1,900 miles of border with Mexico and approximately 95,000 miles of shoreline, CBP is responsible for preventing the illegal movement of people and contraband. CBP's Border Patrol and Air and Marine agents patrol our Nation's land and littoral borders and associated airspace to prevent illegal entry of people and goods into the United States. CBP officers (CBPOs) and agriculture specialists are multi-disciplined and perform the full range of inspection, intelligence analysis, examination, and law enforcement activities relating to the arrival and departure of persons, conveyances, and merchandise at air, land, and sea ports of entry (POEs).

To this end, CBP has significantly developed its intelligence and targeting capabilities to segment and target shipments and individuals according to the level of risk they pose. Beyond managing the influx of people and cargo arriving in the United States, CBP is also working with other DHS agencies to develop a capability to better identify foreign nationals who have violated immigration law, as well as to track suspect persons and cargo exiting the United States. These efforts demonstrate CBP's commitment to developing not only a safer and more secure domestic environment, but also a global one.

Equally important to promoting national and border security, CBP enhances America's economic competitiveness by enabling lawful trade and travel at the Nation's 328 POEs. Efficiently and effectively processing goods and people across U.S. borders is crucial to support the U.S. economy, promote job growth, and help the private sector remain globally competitive, today and in the future. Through better business practices, CBP is advancing its ability to better identify needs and requirements at and between POEs that will enable and facilitate cross-border trade and travel. Through these better business practices, CBP is also streamlining its processing of people and cargo to better align the organization's policies and procedures. As both international trade and travel increase, CBP must increase its capacity to facilitate and secure cross-border activity through better training and enabling technologies, allowing the United States and global economies to grow and prosper.

Service to the Public:

The American people place enormous trust and confidence in CBP to keep them safe and CBP must ensure that its employees maintain the highest professional standards. CBP protects the American public from acts of terrorism by constant vigilance at and between POEs. CBP protects American businesses and workers by ensuring travelers and goods move safely and efficiently across our borders; immigrants and visitors are properly documented; and customs, immigration, and trade laws, regulations, and agreements are enforced.

FY 2014 Accomplishments:

Trade Facilitation

- CBP processed more than $2.4 trillion in international trade, an increase of more than 4 percent from FY 2013, while enforcing U.S. trade laws that protect the nation's economy and the health and safety of the American public. CBP processed more than 31 million imports. Duty collection remains a CBP priority and the agency collected $43.5 billion from duties, taxes, and fees in FY 2014. In addition, CBP processed more than $1.6 trillion worth of U.S. exported goods, an increase of 4 percent from the previous fiscal year.

- CBP processed more than 25.7 million cargo containers through the nation's ports of entry, up 4.5 percent from last fiscal year. CBP conducted more than 23,161 seizures of goods that violated intellectual property rights, with a total retail value of $1.2 billion.

A Radiation Portal Monitor is used to inspect a shipping container for contraband.

- CBP deployed a fully automated export manifest to the air and sea environments. This solution will reduce costs to the trade community by over $50 million by reducing the cost of copying documents and courier fees. The automated export manifest will also reduce CBP storage, labor, and transportation costs by over $3 million per year.

- CBP installed Automated Passport Control kiosks in 22 locations in FY 2014 to streamline the traveler inspection process, reduce wait times, and enhance security. At some APC locations, wait times decreased by as much as 25-40 percent.

Travel Promotion

- CBPOs at 328 POEs inspected more than 374 million travelers in FY 2014, an increase of 4 percent from the previous fiscal year. More than 107 million international travelers arrived at U.S. air ports of entry, an increase of 4.7 percent from the previous fiscal year. Despite the continued increase in international air travelers, average wait times were down 13 percent at the top 10 air ports of entry. At John F. Kennedy International Airport, the airport with the most passenger volume in the United States, the average wait time for FY 2014 was 22 minutes, down 28 percent from FY 2013.

- CBP's Trusted Traveler Programs reached record numbers of enrollment in FY 2014. An additional 1.25 million people enrolled in the agency's Trusted Traveler Programs (Global Entry, SENTRI, NEXUS and FAST) this fiscal year to bring total enrollment to more than 3.3 million members. Global Entry, the agency's largest program with more than 1.7 million members, is operational at 42 U.S. airports and 12 Preclearance locations, serving 99 percent of incoming travelers to the United States. CBP added nine Global Entry kiosk locations this fiscal year and enrolled its one millionth member in NEXUS.

A traveler uses a Global Entry kiosk at Miami International Airport.

- In FY 2014, CBP expanded Preclearance operations to a 15th location, Abu Dhabi International Airport. More than 16 million travelers went through one of CBP's Preclearance locations in Canada, Ireland, the Caribbean, and the United Arab Emirates in FY 2014, accounting for 15 percent of total international air travel volume for FY 2014. Preclearance allows for the inspection process to occur on foreign soil prior to boarding a direct flight to the United States, without further CBP processing or security screening on arrival. This saves passengers' time, reduces wait times, increases capacity for airlines, and allows the United States and our international partners to jointly identify and address threats at the earliest possible point.

- In FY 2014, CBP coordinated with other Federal agencies to respond to the international spread of the Ebola virus. CBP efforts related to Ebola include advanced screening of travelers from Ebola-infected regions, additional passenger targeting operations, purchases of Personal Protective Equipment (PPE) for CBP agents and officers, and Ebola response training courses.

Enforcement

- Border Patrol apprehensions totaled 486,651 nationwide in FY 2014, compared to 420,789 last year. The uptick is largely due to the increase in unaccompanied children and family units who turned themselves in to Border Patrol agents in South Texas this summer. In FY 2013, the U.S. Border Patrol apprehended a total of 38,833 unaccompanied children and 15,056 family units nationwide. In FY 2014, those numbers were 68,631 and 68,684, respectively – a 76 percent increase in unaccompanied children and a 356 percent increase in family units over FY 2013. DHS and other Federal agencies responded aggressively to this spike, and as a result, the number of unaccompanied children currently entering is significantly lower than this time last year.

A Border Patrol Agent scans the area along the Rio Grande for potential inadmissible aliens staging to enter into the United States illegally.

- At ports of entry in FY 2014, CBPOs arrested 8,013 individuals wanted for serious crimes. Officers also stopped 223,712 inadmissible aliens from entering the United States through ports of entry, an increase of 9.25 percent from FY 2013. Grounds of inadmissibility include immigration violations, criminal and related violations, and national security and related grounds. Depending on the circumstances, these individuals were arrested, allowed to voluntarily return to their country of origin, or allowed to withdraw their application for admission into the United States.

- CBP agriculture specialists seized 1.6 million prohibited plant materials, meat, and animal byproducts in FY 2014, and intercepted nearly 155,000 pests at POEs.

A member of the CBP Beagle Brigade searches for prohibited agricultural products and meats brought in by arriving passengers.

- CBP officers and agents seized more than 3.8 million pounds of narcotics across the country in FY 2014. In addition, the agency seized more than $237 million in unreported currency through targeted enforcement operations. During FY 2014, P-3 aircrews from Corpus Christi, Texas, and Jacksonville, Florida, detected 149 suspected smuggling vessels and aircraft. This led to DHS's seizure of 112,224 pounds of cocaine with an estimated street value of more than $8.4 billion.

- CBP fully implemented the Flight Dashboard, a joint initiative between CBP and the Transportation Security Administration (TSA) to share data on identified No Fly List and Terrorist Screening Database (TSDB) matches in a real-time visual format, which involves integrating CBP and TSA vetting results into one dashboard to provide both agencies with a common operating picture.

- CBP air and marine agents achieved a total of 90,740 flight hours and 104,811 float hours.

- CBP adapted new sensor technologies across CBP's nine Unmanned Aircraft Systems, increasing their effectiveness and flexibility along the land borders, maritime approaches, and source/transit zones.

A CBP Unmanned Aircraft System (UAS) conducts surveillance operations over the Southwest Border.

- As part of its commitment to transparency, CBP publicly released the revised Use of Force Policy handbook and a consultant study on use of force in May 2014. Additionally, CBP is testing less lethal options, with enhanced range capabilities, to alter the threat perception by CBP agents and officers and provide agents and officers with other safe tactics designed to minimize injury to officers or other persons.

- In FY 2014, CBP began to implement a unified, formal review process for use of force incidents. This process will create a unified approach to effectively respond to and investigate use of force incidents in a timely manner. Additionally, as part of the process, an interagency board will review use of force incidents to determine compliance with policy and best law enforcement practices for training, tactics, and equipment. CBP also formed an Integrity Advisory Panel to provide CBP with best practices and recommendations from federal, state, and local law enforcement integrity thought leaders. CBP also plans to implement a feasibility study of the use of body worn cameras in each of CBP's operational environments along the U.S. border, at and between ports of entry, in the air and at sea.

Legislative Proposal to Increase COBRA and Immigration User Fees (IUF) and Lift the IUF Exemption on Sea Passengers

CBP's FY 2015 Report to Congress on Resource Optimization at POEs will include the results of the Workload Staffing Model (WSM) – the primary tool used by CBP to inform staffing decisions at POEs. The WSM identified a need for additional workforce capacity at our POEs today, assuming current processes, procedures, technology, facilities, and use of overtime. The 2,000 new CBPOs funded in the FY 2014 Omnibus will help address the current gap in capabilities. Additionally, the WSM projects the need for additional staff in FY 2016 due to expanding facilities, technology deployments, and expected growth in travel and trade. Combined, CBP's total additional requirement through FY 2016 is roughly the equivalent of 2,700 CBPOs.

Through a legislative proposal to the appropriate Congressional Authorizing Committees, CBP is proposing an increase of $2.00 to the IUF, bringing the new fee amount to $9.00. The IUF has not been raised since May 2002. Additionally, under the Immigration and Nationality Act, each sea passenger arriving in the United States is currently charged a $7.00 fee if his or her journey originated from a place outside of United States, other than certain, exempt regions. CBP proposes lifting the exemption for passengers traveling from those regions, to include the United States and its territories, so that the same fee will be applied to all sea passengers. Together, the additional revenue collected from these increases will fund up to 1,400 new CBPOs, which will reduce wait times at air and sea POEs, especially as cruise volumes continue to grow as projected in future years.

In addition to the IUF increases, a legislative proposal to the appropriate Congressional Authorizing Committees is proposing to increase COBRA fees (statutorily set under the *Consolidated Omnibus Budget Reconciliation Act of 1985*) and the ECCF fee created under the *Trade Act of 2002*. COBRA created a series of user fees for air and sea passengers, commercial trucks, railroad cars, private aircraft and vessels, commercial vessels, dutiable mail packages, broker permits, barges and bulk carriers from Canada and Mexico, cruise vessel passengers, and ferry vessel passengers. This proposal would increase the current commercial aircraft and vessel passenger fee by $2.00, bringing the new fee amount to $7.50, and increase other COBRA fees by a proportional amount. The ECCF fee was created to reimburse CBP for inspection costs related to express consignment and the proposal would increase the current fee by $0.36. The additional revenue raised from these fee increases will allow CBP to recover more costs associated with customs-related inspections, and reduce wait times by supporting the hiring of up to 900 new CBPOs.

BUDGET REQUEST

Dollars in Thousands

	FY 2014 Revised Enacted		FY 2015 President's Budget		FY 2016 President's Budget		FY 2016 +/- FY 2015	
	FTE	$0	FTE	$0	FTE	$0	FTE	$0
Headquarters Management and Administration	3,070	1,212,598	3,298	1,183,722	3,327	1,506,012	29	322,290
Border Security Inspections and Trade Facilitation at POEs	20,512	3,198,005	20,672	3,204,041	21,381	3,560,360	709	356,319
Border Security and Control Between the POEs	23,118	3,681,969	23,166	3,938,623	23,166	4,003,307	0	64,684
Subtotal, Salaries & Expenses	**46,700**	**8,092,572**	**47,136**	**8,326,386**	**47,874**	**9,069,679**	**738**	**743,293**
Air and Marine Interdiction, Salaries and Expenses, Operations, Maintenance, and Procurement	1,711	805,068	1,719	708,685	1,734	747,422	15	38,737
Automation Modernization	1,462	854,830	1,578	812,410	1,620	867,311	42	54,901
Facilities Management	483	472,778	486	482,205	386	341,543	-100	-140,662
Border Security Fencing, Infrastructure, and Technology	0	351,454	0	362,466	0	373,461	0	10,995
COBRA FTA	1,284	175,000	1,284	180,000	1,284	180,000	0	0
COBRA	0	0	0	0	0	0	0	0
IUF	0	0	0	0	0	0	0	0
Small Airports	69	8,533	69	8,789	69	9,097	0	308
Global Entry	96	34,835	96	91,192	96	91,789	0	597
Offsetting Collections	0	0	0	0	0	0	0	0
Gross Discretionary	**51,805**	**10,795,070**	**52,368**	**10,972,133**	**53,063**	**11,680,302**	**695**	**708,169**
Customs Unclaimed Goods	0	6,135	0	5,992	0	5,992	0	0
Mandatory/Fees	9,091	1,662,688	9,339	1,786,710	9,389	1,879,000	50	92,290
Total Budget Authority	**60,896**	**12,463,893**	**61,707**	**12,764,835**	**62,452**	**13,565,294**	**745**	**800,459**
Add Supplemental Funding	0	0	0	0	0	0	0	0
Less prior year Rescissions	0	($68,297)	0	0	0	0	0	0
Total	**60,896**	**12,395,596**	**61,707**	**12,764,835**	**62,452**	**13,565,294**	**745**	**800,459**

FY 2016 Highlights:

- **Non-Intrusive Inspection (NII) Equipment Refresh & Recapitalization ......$85.3M (0 FTE)**
  The budget provides an increase of $85.3 million for the NII program. The requested increase will fund recapitalization of aging systems, which currently include 314 large scale and 4,930 small scale systems. Without this funding increase, maintenance costs would rise, systems would become obsolete, system downtime would rise impacting the effectiveness of inspections, labor costs would increase, and the movement of legitimate trade and travel would be delayed due to the need for manual inspections. In FY 2014, CBP conducted over 7.2 million NII examinations. Of these examinations, over 2.3 million inspections were for cargo truck and seaport containers using imaging technology. Relying solely on physical inspections would have required an increase in staff by over 8,000 officers to manage the workload. When compared to a physical search, the time it takes to conduct a secondary examination is reduced by an average of 112 minutes, from 2 hours to 8 minutes for a team of 3 officers. This equates to approximately 13 million hours in time savings.

- **Facilities Management & Sustainment ....$78.8M (0 FTE)**
  The budget provides $78.8 million for CBP's real property portfolio maintenance and repair backlog. At the end of FY 2014, based on Facility Condition Assessments (FCA) at CBP-owned and Direct Lease Operated facilities, CBP documented a large backlog of unmet maintenance and repair requirements. This backlog includes significant life safety and security issues for CBP personnel and the general public, along with systems that are at high risk of failure, which will potentially cause interruptions to the successful execution of CBP's mission and operations. The funding increase will remediate life safety and security requirements and repair facility deficiencies, improving operational capabilities and workplace quality. The funds will also be used to support installation or upgrade of security systems and other requirements at leased facilities. These costs are incurred as a result of mandatory relocations or are required to address security vulnerabilities and deficiencies upon renewal of existing occupancy agreements. CBP will apply a prioritization approach to allocate the $78.8 million to address the most critical CBP facilities infrastructure requirements, with the ultimate goal of ensuring that CBP facilities are safe working environments that allow CBP to efficiently execute each one of its strategic mission areas.

- **Arizona Tactical Infrastructure... $44.7M (0 FTE)**
  The budget provides funding for CBP to complete the Naco Primary Fence Replacement Project. This Project is a high priority fence project for the United States Border Patrol (USBP) along the southwest border and involves the removal and replacement of an estimated 7.5 miles of existing primary pedestrian fence in Zone 30. This section of fence has been successfully exploited by Transnational Criminal Organizations (TCO) due to ease of concealment (the fence is within a populated area) and due to the inadequate design of the fence (the fence lacks adequate height, foundation, and strength). The funding requested will address these vulnerabilities.

- **King Air (KA)-350CER Multi-Role Enforcement Aircraft (MEA) .... $44.4M (0 FTE)**
  The budget provides an increase of $44.4 million for two KA-350CER MEAs. The MEA is a multi-role enforcement aircraft with a multi-mode radar for use over water and land, and for air-to-air situational awareness. It is the most capable new, twin-engine aircraft that CBP has purchased and is a critical investment to support Border Patrol agents and improve air-to-ground surveillance capabilities.

- **Revenue Modernization** .... **$12.6M (0 FTE)**
  The budget provides $12.6 million additional funds for Revenue Modernization in FY 2016, which will be directed toward prioritizing the transition of select revenue collections from the POEs, reengineering complex collections business processes, and enhancing financial reporting functionality through automation. In addition, funding will be used to develop and deploy electronic payment capability (e.g., payments via mobile apps and kiosks).

  Revenue Modernization will allow CBP to consolidate, automate, and streamline fragmented and manual processes by leveraging modern technology to safeguard over $48 billion in annual collections used throughout the Federal Government to support critical programs, and promote U.S. Trade and Travel. Specifically, Revenue Modernization will incrementally:

  - ○ Create operational efficiencies at the Ports of Entry (POEs) by allowing CBP Officers to focus more on critical security and compliance issues;

  - ○ Benefit the trade and travel industry and the U.S. economy by providing modern electronic billing and payment options;

  - ○ Support CBP customs enforcement and Revenue back office operations by enhancing the speed, accuracy, and controls over collections through direct, electronic deposits; and

  - ○ Enable access to real-time, reliable financial and operational data to inform decision-making and comply with existing and emerging reporting requirements from Treasury, Congress, DHS, and OMB.

- **Flight Hour Increase** .... **$32.5M (0 FTE)**
  The budget provides $32.5 million for an increase of over 16,500 CBP flight hours to achieve a total of 91,373 total flight hours based on the current planned flight hour allocation, which will support the highest priority operations along the southwest border and within the drug source and transit zones. The funds would be used primarily for fuel but also includes materiel (parts, consumable supplies, contracts for the repair of repairables), planned and unplanned maintenance and operational travel for OAM and contract support personnel. The funding provides for all aircraft types that support southwest border operations and operations within the source, transit, and arrival zones, including the P-3 and DSH-8 aircraft.

- **Electronic Visa Information Update System (EVIUS)** .... **$29.4M (5 FTE)**
  The budget provides an increase of $29.4 million for EVIUS. This new program will allow non-immigrant visa (NIV) holders to provide updated biographic and travel-related information through a public website. This process will enable CBP to facilitate admissibility determinations post-visa issuance before passengers initiate travel to the United States. The system will complement the existing visa application process and enhance CBP's ability to make pre-travel risk determinations. CBP proposes piloting this program for travelers from China who are issued 10-year, multiple entry B1, B2, or B1/B2 visas for business and tourism. The program will require travelers with these visas to provide updated biographic and travel information to CBP via a public website every 2 years

from the date of visa issuance for the duration of visa validity. CBP will review and adjudicate the updated biographic and travel-related information to support admissibility determinations and facilitate processing upon arrival in the United States.

- **Unaccompanied Children (UC) Funding** .... **$29.1M (0 FTE)**
  The budget provides up to $29.1 million for costs associated with apprehension and care of up to 104,000 UCs. During FY 2014, the southwest border experienced an unprecedented increase in the number of UCs crossing the border. Due to the volume of children crossing the border, CBP maintained custody of UCs for a much longer period of time than originally planned. Their overall numbers and the duration of their detention required CBP to take additional measures to provide adequate care for UCs. These measures included contracting with outside vendors to provide food services, showers and laundry services for health hygiene, monitoring, medical care, and the purchase of significant amounts of personal hygiene items. CBP has developed a contingency plan to deal with the situation in the future should the numbers of UCs exceed historic levels. Up to $134.5 million in contingency funding authority would be used to provide the necessary support activities required to apprehend and maintain the health and safety of the UCs once specific threshold levels are met. Because of the low probability of such a high number of UCs attempting to enter the United States in FY 2016, the Budget scores the requested increase at $24.4 million. An additional $4.7 million will be utilized for supplies for UCs at Border Patrol (BP) Stations and Land Ports of Entry (LPOEs). This requested funding will be used to procure a standardized set of supplies and personal hygiene items that will be provided to mothers and unaccompanied children at BP stations and LPOEs.

- **Mobile Surveillance Capability (MSC)** .... **$16.0M (0 FTE)**
  The budget provides funding to procure a minimum of 10 MSC systems, including initial spares and program support, for deployment to the El Paso, Big Bend, and Del Rio Sectors. CBP may be able to procure additional MSC systems depending on the costs associated with procuring initial spares and program support. The maximum procurement that CBP anticipates with the funding provided is 19 systems.

- **Establish Counter Network Operations** .... **$14.7M (60 FTE)**
  The budget establishes a counter network capability and augments the existing Automated Targeting System (ATS) to provide enhanced capabilities. These resources will support a collaborative analytic environment with access to the necessary data and tools to conduct advanced counter network analysis of the nation's key transnational organized crime and terrorist targets. Undetected criminal and terrorist travel, contraband movement, and commercial and financial activity necessitates continued improvement in our ability to uncover the patterns and faint signals that exist within disparate sources of information. $10.9 million of the requested funding amount will support the additional 60 FTEs at the National Targeting Center and the remaining $3.8 million will provide contractor and information technology support to the ATS.

- **Intelligence & Targeting Operations** .... **$12.9M (24 FTE)**
  The budget provides funding to support hardware, software, and network updates to the Automated Targeting System (ATS), expand existing infrastructure, increase bandwidth, upgrade the Data Warehouse and Enterprise Reporting System, and allow the strategic build out of an additional three (3) Intelligence Support Teams (IST). The additional funding will permit the Field Support Division to provide cutting edge support to CBP field activities and

the organizations that partner with them through the deployment of tailored intelligence support teams and will prevent degradation of older critical infrastructure that supports ATS operations. The personnel supported by this increase would comprise three additional intelligence support teams that would be deployed to the California Corridor Campaign, Florida, and the Pacific Northwest Campaign.

- **Border Security Deployment Program (BSDP)...$11.1M (0 FTE)** The budget provides an increase of $11.1 million for BDSP. BSDP provides CBP with a comprehensive and expanded secure operational environment through an integrated surveillance and intrusion detection system that delivers critical security, motion detection, remote monitoring, and situational awareness for all LPOEs. BSDP is a mission critical tool for the LPOEs where CBP officers and agents use security, surveillance, and audio systems on a 24x7 basis. BSDP improves the safety and security of CBP officers, the traveling public, and government facilities. BSDP also promotes officer integrity, and adjudicates judicial investigations through court admissible video and audio recordings. BSDP, as a force multiplier, allows CBP officers and agents to focus their attention on the efficient flow of people and goods at the border. BSDP situational awareness at LPOEs is also used to monitor the overall operations at LPOEs and make real-time efficiency and risk adjustments as needed.

- **Canine Enforcement Program (CEP) ....$10.0M (23 FTE)** The budget provides an increase of $10.0 million for its CEP. The CEP plays a crucial role in anti-terrorism and interdiction efforts. Through the CEP, CBP has established and deployed a world-class detector dog program to augment existing technology while employing cutting edge detection capabilities. The Office of Field Operations (OFO) canine teams are strategically assigned to POEs around the United States and to preclearance operations abroad. This increase will result in a total of 47 more canine teams, with a mix of Currency/Firearms and Human/Narcotics Detection, deployed to the POEs with the highest need. Below is a breakout of these additional 47 teams by port:

Field Office	Currency/Firearms	Human/Narcotics Detection	Total
Atlanta	1	1	2
Baltimore	2	2	4
Boston	1	1	2
Chicago	0	2	2
Detroit	1	1	2
El Paso	0	2	2
Houston	0	1	1
Laredo	1	7	8
Los Angeles	0	1	1
Miami/Tampa	1	1	2
New York	1	1	2
San Diego	1	5	6
Tucson	4	9	13
TOTAL	**13**	**34**	**47**

Of this requested increase, $360,000 will be used by Office of Border Patrol to increase the number of canines to eventually meet its requirement for 1,115 canines. Canines are used to detect illegal aliens, illegal drugs, and illegal currency at checkpoints and are used in field operations to track and apprehend illegal aliens.

- **High Risk Internal Cybersecurity Remediation** .... **$9.0M (0 FTE)**
  As part of a DHS-wide initiative, the budget provides an increase of $9.0 million to implement High Risk Internal Cybersecurity remediation actions of CBPs information technology systems in accordance with the DHS initiative. The additional funding will enable CBP to actively pursue the closure of highest priority FY 2015 known cybersecurity system vulnerabilities and initiate actions to ensure that information technology systems are retained above acceptable standards.

- **Unmanned Aircraft Systems (UAS) Crew** .... **$8.4M (15 FTE)**
  The budget provides $8.4 million for an additional 15 UAS crew in support of operations along the southwest border and operations within the source and transit zone. The 15 additional UAS crew will include eight Air Interdiction Agents; four Sensor Operators; three support staff positions; and the necessary salaries, benefits, overtime, premium pay, training, travel, law enforcement equipment, and supplies. The positions are needed to provide increased CBP aerial surveillance, enforcement, and security posture for surges similar to that of unaccompanied children illegally entering the U.S.

- **National Geospatial Border Strategy** .... **$8.4M (0 FTE)**
  The budget provides an increase of $8.4 million supporting the expansion of the National Border Geospatial Intelligence Strategy (NBGIS) to the northern border, equipment refresh for the Law Enforcement Technical Collections (LETC) program in the Caribbean basin, and augmentation of existing Intelligence Support Team (IST) locations participating in

  joint task forces such as the Department of Homeland Security's Southwest Border and Approaches Campaign Plan.

- **Department of Defense (DoD) Equipment Re-Use** .... **$8.5M (0 FTE)**
  The budget provides an increase that will allow CBP to complete the installation, training, operation, and maintenance of re-locatable towers. It will also provide for logistics and sustainment support for aerostat and re-locatable tower deployments, including the utility evaluation, site preparation, and operation of one aerostat. This will also allow CBP to conduct technical evaluations and deploy additional DoD re-use systems to the field. Some of these technologies include: foliage penetrating sensors, night vision detection devices, and wireless sensor data link systems.

- **Replace Legacy MVSS and Agent-Portable Systems in Rio Grande Valley** .... **$2.2M (0 FTE)**
  The budget provides an increase in development and deployment funding for the Mobile Video Surveillance Systems (MVSS) Program and agent-portable systems, which will benefit CBP operations on the southwest border. The MVSS Program will receive $25.020 million in FY 2016 funding, which is $0.371 million over the current services level. This funding will be used for the acquisition of MVSS units and the support staff for the management and deployment throughout Texas. The deployments will satisfy USBP needs

in Laredo, Big Bend, and Del Rio sectors; the MVSS Program also plans to begin deployments to meet operational needs in the El Paso sector. CBP estimates that at least 73 MVSS units will be acquired with the FY 2016 funding requested.

In FY 2016, $1.824 million is requested for the procurement and deployment of agent-portable systems on the Southwest border. CBP will acquire agent-portable technology that is consistent with CBP operational needs.

- **Watchlist Service (WLS) Encounter**..**$1.9M (0 FTE)**
  The budget provide an increase of $1.9 million to develop and implement DHS WLS Encounter Data Broker, which will streamline the return of information obtained by DHS Components from terrorist Watchlist encounters by electronically transmitting the information back to the Terrorist Screening Center (TSC). This funding will increase support for WLS current functions so there is a solid system to build the encounter function upon. DHS WLS fully supports the "One DHS" information sharing directive and the Homeland Security Enterprise Architecture (HLS EA) and, as such, uses the Terrorist Watchlist Person Data Exchange Standard (TWPDES) schema to send and receive information, as well as the DHS Core Biographic Person Data Elements (CBPDE). The next phase of development is the WLS Encounter Data Broker, which will streamline the return of information obtained by DHS Components from terrorist Watchlist encounters by electronically transmitting the information back to the TSC.

- **FAA NextGen Compliance Compliance** ....**$1.6M (0 FTE)**
  The budget provides $1.6 million to support the phased purchase and installation of Automatic Dependent Surveillance-Broadcast (ADS-B) transponders and cockpit displays in all OAM aircraft. The Federal Aviation Administration (FAA) intends to mandate increased ADSB-Out pilot and controller situational awareness in the satellite based NextGen airspace system. The use of ADS–B for aircraft surveillance by FAA and Department of Defense (DOD) air traffic controllers will safely and efficiently accommodate aircraft operations and the expected increase in demand for air transportation.

- **Additional Polygraph Examiners**..**$1.5M (5 FTE)**
  The budget provides an increase of $1.5 million to provide additional support to the Office of Internal Affairs (IA) Credibility Assessment Division (CAD). CAD conducts applicant screening polygraph examinations. This request would provide funding to allow CBP to hiring hire an additional 40 Polygraph Examiners, which will gain program capacity and allow CBP to more effectively comply with the expansion of the Anti-Border Corruption Act 2010 (ABCA), while also allowing CBP to help eliminate a choke-point area within the hiring process.

FY 2016 Major Decreases:

- **Reduction to BSFIT Operations & Maintenance**..**$13.9M (0 FTE)**
  The proposed base adjustment to BSFIT O&M in FY 2016 will capitalize on savings that were generated as a result of the successful Integrated Fixed Towers (IFT) Program contract price negotiations which resulted in lower costs than the approved life-cycle cost estimate. The contract savings for FY 2016 totaled to $22.6 million. The $13.8 million decrease represents the decrease in IFT funding levels from FY 2015 to FY 2016. The IFT savings from BSFIT have been reallocated to other CBP priorities.

- **Delay Vehicle Recapitalization** ....$10.0M (0 FTE)
  CBP proposes a reduction to vehicle acquisition funding of $10 million in FY 2016. Based upon the CBP fleet assessment analysis conducted in FY 2013, CBP identified approximately 6,227 vehicles for reduction from the fleet. Out of these approximate 6,227 vehicles, 4,166 estimated reductions are scheduled to occur between FY 2014 and FY 2015. The remainder 2,061 vehicles will be reduced in FY 2016.

- **Data Center Operations and Maintenance**..$9.2M (0 FTE)
  The Office of Information and Technology (OIT) will seek to achieve savings through the implementation of cloud computing services where feasible, and will continue to seek acquisition strategies and new contracts for support services that provide competitive, lower costs. OIT is also looking at how it acquires and delivers services today, versus how they may be delivered more efficiently in the future. New technology solutions are rapidly being introduced, and OIT will take advantage of emerging technology capabilities that meet CBPs mission requirements, in a secure environment, for reduced cost.

- **Reduction in Manual Continuous Monitoring**...$1.1M (0 FTE)
  The budget decreases $1.1 million in funding for certain information technology cybersecurity applications in favor of automated and standardized cybersecurity programs.

U.S. Immigration and Customs Enforcement

Description:

U.S. Immigration and Customs Enforcement (ICE) is the principal investigative arm of the U.S. Department of Homeland Security (DHS) and the second largest investigative agency in the Federal Government. Created in 2003 through a merger of the U.S. Customs Service and the Immigration and Naturalization Service, ICE has more than 19,000 employees in all 50 states, the District of Columbia, and 48 foreign countries.

ICE promotes DHS' counterterrorism, border security, and public safety mission through criminal and civil enforcement of approximately 400 federal laws governing border control, customs, trade, and immigration.

At a Glance	
Senior Leadership: *Sarah Saldana, Assistant Secretary*	
Established: 2003	
Major Divisions: *Homeland Security Investigations; Enforcement and Removal Operations; Office of the Principal Legal Advisor; Management and Administration*	
Budget Request:	***$6,281,637,000***
Gross Discretionary:	*$5,959,637,000*
Mandatory, Fees, & Trust Fund:	*$322,000,000*
Employees (FTE):	*19,791*

Responsibilities:

ICE disrupts and dismantles transnational criminal organizations that exploit our borders by preventing terrorism and enhancing security, and enforcing and administering our immigration laws. ICE also identifies, apprehends, and removes criminal and other removable aliens from the United States. The agency carries out its mission through three principal operating components: Homeland Security Investigations (HSI), Enforcement and Removal Operations (ERO), and Management and Administration (M&A). Additionally, the Office of the Principal Legal Advisor (OPLA) leads ICE's legal operations and the Office of Professional Responsibility (OPR) investigates allegations of criminal misconduct at ICE and U.S. Customs and Border Protection (CBP).

- HSI's 6,200 criminal investigators conduct transnational criminal investigations to protect the United States against terrorist and other criminal organizations that threaten public safety and national security and bring to justice those seeking to exploit our customs and immigration laws worldwide. HSI uses its legal authorities to investigate immigration and customs violations, including export enforcement, human rights violations, narcotics, weapons and contraband smuggling, financial crimes, cybercrimes, human trafficking and smuggling, child exploitation, intellectual property violations, transnational gangs, and immigration benefit fraud.

- ERO's 5,800 deportation officers and immigration enforcement agents enforce our Nation's immigration laws by identifying and apprehending removable aliens, detaining these individuals when necessary, and removing them from the United States. To protect public safety and national security, ICE prioritizes the removal of individuals who pose a danger to national security or a risk to public safety, including aliens apprehended at the border while attempting to unlawfully enter the United States and aliens convicted of crimes, with particular emphasis on violent criminals, felons, and repeat offenders.

- OPLA's 900 attorneys represent the United States Government in exclusion, deportation, bond, and removal proceedings before the Department of Justice's (DOJ) Executive Office for Immigration Review (EOIR). OPLA attorneys prioritize the litigation of removal hearings that involve criminal aliens, terrorists, and human rights abusers, as well as other priorities for enforcement. OPLA also provides critical legal advice to ICE's law enforcement components that focus on criminal and administrative customs and immigration offenses. OPLA provides general legal advice regarding fiscal and procurement law, ethics, information disclosure, employment and labor law, federal litigation, and other administrative matters. OPLA attorneys support the DOJ in defending removal orders when they are appealed to the U.S. Courts of Appeals and the U.S. Supreme Court. In addition, OPLA attorneys, as Special Assistant U.S. Attorneys (SAUSA), prosecute criminal immigration and customs cases in federal court.

- M&A provides the full range of mission and operational support for ICE's program offices. M&A manages ICE's financial and human resources, information technology, sensitive property, and other assets. M&A ensures collaboration with internal and external stakeholders to increase ICE's ability to attract and retain a diverse workforce. M&A also processes over 30,000 Freedom of Information Act (FOIA) requests each year, provides firearms and tactical training to over 6,000 special agents and officers, trains new and existing ICE employees, and procures goods and services for the agency.

- The Office of Professional Responsibility (OPR) upholds the agency's standards for integrity and professionalism. As a key part of that responsibility, OPR investigates allegations of misconduct involving employees of ICE and U.S. Customs and Border Protection (CBP). OPR also provides independent reviews of ICE programs and offices, adjudicates ICE background investigations and issues security clearances for all prospective and current ICE employees and contract staff. In addition, OPR inspects and reviews ICE offices, operations and processes in an effort to provide executive management with an independent review of the agency's organizational health. OPR oversees the agency's detention functions to ensure compliance with ICE detention standards.

Service to the Public:

HSI New York Deputy Special Agent in Charge Tony Scandiffio, speaking, and Suffolk County District Attorney Thomas Spota announce the indictment of 19 people on cocaine trafficking charges

In Fiscal Year (FY) 2014, ICE made 38,812 criminal arrests while seizing $720 million in U.S. currency and other monetary instruments, 1.3 million pounds of narcotics and other dangerous drugs, and 35,346 weapons. ICE responded to 1,450,732 alienage inquiries from other federal, state, and local law enforcement agencies through ICE's Law Enforcement Support Center. Additionally, ICE removed 315,943 illegal aliens, of which 98 percent fell into one of ICE's immigration enforcement priorities (criminal aliens, repeat immigration violators, and recent border crossers).

FY 2014 Accomplishments:

Homeland Security Investigations

In FY 2014, HSI's criminal investigators targeted transnational criminal enterprises seeking to exploit America's legitimate trade, travel, and financial system. Last year, HSI arrested 46,965 individuals, making 32,259 criminal arrests and 14,706 administrative arrests. HSI also conducted 1,327 I-9 inspections; issued 638 Final Orders for more than $16 million in fines; initiated 1,656 intellectual property rights (IPR) investigations; and identified and assisted more than 2,300 crime victims, including 446 human trafficking victims and 1,036 child exploitation victims.

Highlights

- ICE launched Operation Coyote to address the extraordinarily high volume of human smuggling activity in the Rio Grande Valley area of Texas by deploying 60 additional personnel to the region. In its first 90 days, agents initiated 313 human smuggling investigations, leading to 676 criminal arrests, 403 indictments, and 240 convictions. The operation netted the seizures of 25 firearms, 78 vehicles, and over $43,250.

- In FY 2014, ICE identified and dismantled eight alien smuggling organizations, including the Chuky alien smuggling organization in Guatemala and the Diaz-Perdomo alien smuggling organization in El Salvador. The operation resulted in the arrest of 37 alien smuggling organization members, and seizures of $1.5 million, 26 weapons, 16 vehicles, and 33 properties valued at approximately $1 million.

- ICE continued to work with its law enforcement partners to identify and apprehend criminal elements. In FY 2014, ICE collaborated with 150 federal, state, and local law enforcement agencies from 179 cities in Project Southbound to apprehend 757 criminals. Of those apprehended, 638 were gang members and associates from 145 gangs, including 256 foreign nationals from 21 countries. ICE also seized 54 firearms, over 100 pounds of narcotics, over $166,000, and 10 vehicles during the operation.

- ICE continued its support and participation in the World Customs Organization's Program Global Shield (PGS), a multilateral law enforcement program that shares information on global movement of 14 precursor chemicals used to manufacture improvised explosive devices (IEDs). In FY 2014, ICE's participation resulted in 124 seizures of approximately 332 metric tons of precursor materials and 72 IEDs.

- ICE's Office of International Affairs partners with foreign and domestic counterparts to conduct international law enforcement operations. In FY 2014, ICE conducted an investigation in Panama which resulted in the United Nations (U.N.) and the U.S. Department of Treasury imposing sanctions on the Ocean Maritime Management Company and 18 associated vessels, including the Chon Chong Gang. The investigation also led to the discovery of 240 tons of munitions, radar equipment, and two MiG fighter jets – the largest amount of arms and related material interdicted to or from the Democratic People's Republic of Korea since the adoption of United Nations Security Council Resolution 1718 in 2006, according to the U.N.

- In FY 2014, ICE repatriated 32 cultural artifacts to eight countries and two museums. Among the repatriations were nine royal seals of the Korean Empire and Joseon Dynasty to the Republic of Korea, which coincided with President Obama's visit to Seoul, Korea. This event led to the signing of a Memorandum of Understanding with the Republic of Korea's Cultural Heritage Administration and ICE's Homeland Security Investigations. This MOU is the first of its kind, signed between a U.S. agency and an agency from the Republic of Korea.

- ICE identified and assisted more than 2,300 crime victims from HSI investigations including 446 human trafficking victims and 1,036 child exploitation victims. In addition to victim assistance, referrals for forensic interviews of victims increased over 65 percent and the number of forensic interviews conducted increased 90 percent in FY 2014.

- ICE continued the Visa Security Program modernization project by deploying the Pre-Adjudicated Threat Recognition Intelligence Operations Team (PATRIOT) system to all Visa Security Units, resulting in 100 percent screening of non-immigrant visas at those posts. The implementation of the PATRIOT system also provides the opportunity for additional coordination with U.S. partners earlier in the visa application process.

- In FY 2014, ICE's Student Exchange and Visitor Program (SEVP) reviewed 1,092 academic institutions for possible identification of fraud anomalies; referred 161 academic schools, 2 flight schools, and 3,555 leads on SEVIS violators to HSI field offices for criminal investigation; and recruited 30 of 60 field representatives to improve customer assistance to students and academic institutions seeking recertification and to establish a culture of compliance within the SEVP user community.

- In FY 2014, an independent auditor hired by the DHS Office of the Chief Financial Officer released a final draft of their report giving the Significant Case Review (SCR) process a perfect score for each of the 12 criteria examined. The SCR is conducted by a panel, which reviews enforcement actions and examines the criminal investigative elements that are being presented to ensure that it meets the requirement of a disruption or dismantlement. The auditors expressed that in the history of doing these audits for DHS (since 2009) no entity has ever received a perfect score until the SCR audit.

Enforcement and Removal Operations

In FY 2014, ERO removed 315,943 individuals, of which 98 percent fell into one of ICE's immigration enforcement priorities (criminal aliens, repeat immigration violators, and recent border crossers). Of these removals, 56 percent (177,960) were convicted criminal aliens. This includes 63,159 Level 1 criminal aliens (aliens convicted of crimes such as homicide, rape, and kidnapping). There were approximately 1.9 million aliens on the non-detained docket at the end of FY 2014. This includes 46 percent with a final order of removal.

Highlights

- In the spring and summer of FY 2014, an unprecedented number of unaccompanied children (UC) and adults with children from Central America crossed the southwest border. ICE created a temporary facility in Artesia, New Mexico and converted the Karnes Civil Detention Center to a family residential center to house and expedite the removal of adults with children in a humane manner that complied with federal law and provided for the safety, security, and medical needs of all occupants. In addition, ERO expanded its family residential facilities from one in Berks, PA to locations in Karnes, TX, and Dilley, TX. The Dilley, TX location opened on December 19, 2014, and will house up to 2,072 individuals. The family residential facilities are projected to house approximately 2,760 individuals in total. ERO also transferred 55,488 UC's to Health and Human Services (HHS), its highest number ever. In FY 2014, ICE repatriated 1,901 UC to their country of origin.

- During the month long Operation Cross Check that ran from mid-May to mid-June, ICE ERO officers arrested 297 criminal aliens, fugitives, and other immigration violators in six states. The 287 men and 10 women arrested were from 29 countries and had criminal convictions including arson, domestic abuse, burglary, weapons possession, and sexual assault. During the operation, ICE received assistance from the Department of State, CBP, U.S. Marshals Service, and the Kane County Sheriff's Office.

- ERO successfully expanded the Criminal History Information Sharing (CHIS) program to three additional countries: El Salvador, Guatemala, and Honduras, to improve the sharing of law enforcement data, enhancing the security of the partner country and the U.S. CHIS is a vital international public safety tool that provides participating nations with criminal history information in advance of an alien's removal. CHIS also facilitates the exchange of foreign conviction data to ICE that would have previously gone unknown. These records assist ICE in the identification and classification of additional aliens within the agency's criminal removal priorities.

Office of the Principal Legal Advisor

In FY 2014, as the U.S. Government representative in immigration proceedings, OPLA litigated over 300,000 immigration-related cases before EOIR. Further, OPLA embedded attorneys within HSI and ERO to provide those programs with legal advice and counsel on operational matters as well as labor and employment law issues.

Highlights

- In FY 2014, OPLA assigned 29 attorneys to SAUSA positions, which resulted in over 1,600 criminal convictions in federal court. SAUSAs increase the number of criminals prosecuted for violating immigration and customs laws; aid ICE agents and officers with investigating such crimes; and expedite the removal of criminal aliens. The percentage of removal orders secured by ICE attorneys supporting ICE's civil enforcement priorities (CEP) was 58 percent.

- ICE finished deployment and training on the new case management system (PLAnet) both in the field and at headquarters, which allows for a more accurate accounting of a wide variety of cases and work passing through OPLA at any given time.

- OPLA continued the organization-wide effort to efficiently and effectively handle cases pending on immigration court dockets across the country impacted heavily by the surge of cases along the Rio Grande Valley this spring and summer.

- ICE executed a Memorandum of Understanding and Project Plan with National Technical Information Service to procure a new online reporting system to process the Confidential Financial Disclosure form. The new system will enhance the agency's accountability, compliance, and efficiency by improving the process for tracking and monitoring reporting compliance for the forms.

Management and Administration

M&A provides a full-range of mission and operational support to ICE, including financial management, IT support, law enforcement training, and policy management. In FY 2014, ICE was the first federal law enforcement agency to receive Federal Law Enforcement Training Accreditation for Supervisory Leadership Training. Additionally, ICE processed 33,644 FOIA requests, 427 FOIA appeals, and 39 FOIA litigation cases.

Highlights

- In FY 2014, ICE began developing a new repeatable, evidence-based resource management approach, which employs a three-pronged strategy, to tie workload to resource requirements. The Workload Staffing Model (WSM) uses workload capacity to determine appropriate staffing levels and funding requirements. This approach will provide ICE with the ability to better defend its resource requirements and the resource distribution across ICE programs. WSM allows ICE to justify its staffing requirements and models the impact those resources have on Public Safety, National Security, and the U.S. economy.

- ICE continued to find efficiencies and cost-savings measures in its acquisition of ammunition for its law enforcement officers. In FY 2014, ICE reduced ammunition expenditures by $714,487 from FY 2013 due to enhanced ammunition accountability processes including ammunition inventory verifications, annual physical inventory and FACTS inventory system updates that enhanced controls over ammunition distribution, inventory, and consumption.

- ICE conducted an Electronic Vehicle Allocation Methodology (eVAM) study that identified 478 vehicles that could be removed from the ICE fleet for a potential savings of nearly $2 million. The study also identified over one third of the ICE fleet that could be replaced with less costly vehicles for a potential savings of nearly $4.9 million.

Office of Professional Responsibility

OPR investigates allegations of misconduct involving employees and contractors of ICE, CBP and USCIS; conducts independent inspections of ICE operations; and, manages the personnel and physical security for ICE employees and facilities. In FY 2014, OPR completed 32 detention facility inspections, 18 reviews of 287(g) programs, 17 management inspections, and 25 audits of certified undercover operations.

Highlights

- OPR adjudicated 7,884 enter-on-duty, suitability and security clearance cases, and processed 21,526 customer service/ industrial security determinations.

- In response to influx of unaccompanied children, OPR conducted a compliance inspection of Karnes County Residential Center, where a significant number of families are detained, using the Family Residential Standards.

- OPR investigated and closed 1,148 cases, which included cases on ICE, CBP and CIS employees, civilians, and unknown subjects, as well as cases which were initiated in prior fiscal years. These investigations led to 28 arrests, 17 indictments and 29 convictions. In addition, OPR completed 92% of ICE employee administrative misconduct cases within 180 days and delivered over 110 Integrity Awareness presentations to nearly 2,400 ICE employees.

- OPR collaborated with several DHS and ICE stakeholders to manage the effects of the USIS data breach that affected 27,000 DHS employees, as well as 4,747 ICE employees and contractors. ICE worked closely with Privacy, Acquisitions, Security, and the Chief

- Information Security Officer among others to stay abreast of the data breach. The agency provided the DHS Chief Security Officer with 82 ICE investigative and security personnel to back up the DHS Surge Force in support of background investigations during the work stoppage at OPM and USIS.

BUDGET REQUEST
Dollars in Thousands

	FY 2014 Revised Enacted[1]		FY 2015 President's Budget		FY 2016 President's Budget		FY 2016 +/- FY 2015	
	FTE	$000	FTE	$000	FTE	$000	FTE	$000
Salaries and Expenses	18,977	$5,563,261	19,019	$4,988,065	19,436	$5,881,137	417	$893,072
Automation Modernization	-	34,900	-	26,000	-	73,500	-	47,500
Construction	-	5,000	-	-	-	5,000	-	5,000
Gross Discretionary	**18,977**	**$5,603,161**	**19,019**	**$5,014,065**	**19,436**	**$5,959,637**	**417**	**$945,572**
Mandatory Fees	355	345,000	355	345,000	355	322,000	-	(23,000)
Emergency/ Supplemental	-		-		-		-	
Total Budget Authority	**19,332**	**$5,948,161**	**19,374**	**$5,359,065**	**19,791**	**$6,281,637**	**417**	**$922,572**
Less prior year Rescissions	-	(3,698)	-	-	-	-	-	-
Total	**19,332**	**$5,944,463**	**19,374**	**5,359,065**	**19,791**	**$6,281,637**	**417**	**$922,572**

[1] The FY 2014 Revised Enacted amount for the Salaries and Expenses appropriation includes a transfer of $333,800,000 for Custody Operations ($261.1M) and Transportation and Removal Program($72.7M) for costs associated with unaccompanied children and adults with children. The transfers are from the following DHS accounts: Transportation Security Administration $34,700,000, United States Coast Guard $31,500,000, Federal Emergency Management Agency $267,600,000, as approved by the House and Senate Committees on Appropriations on August 6, 2014, and August 4, 2014, respectively.

FY 2016 Highlights

ICE requests program changes for the Salaries and Expenses appropriation in the following key areas:

- **Increase in new attorney positions** ....**$36.5M (197 FTE)**
  The request will provide funds for 82 attorney positions previously requested in the October 2014 Technical Assistance package and 229 new attorney positions. OPLA requires additional attorney resources to meet its increasing workload driven by recent increases in the number of Department of Justice (DOJ) immigration judges (IJs) and ongoing southwest border surge operations as well as additional requirements anticipated as a result of an increase in Freedom of Information Act (FOIA) requests and appeals. These additional positions are expected to decrease the average length of stay of detainees by 14 percent.

- **Increase in Detention Beds to 34,040** ....**$435.4M (0 FTE)**
  To meet operational needs to detain and remove both criminal aliens and recent border entrants, ICE requests an increase in the overall funding for beds to meet operational needs. The proposed increase will fund 31,280 adult beds at an average rate of $123.54 and 2,760 individuals housed in family units at an average rate of $342.73 from ICE's discretionary appropriation and fees.

- **Alternatives to Detention (ATD)** ....$30.8 M (0 FTE)
  The funding increase will provide for additional ATD full-service capacity to accommodate individuals in family units who are released from custody pursuant to ICE policy or by an immigration judge, and placed on the non-detained court docket. It is estimated that this funding level will fund a total 53,000 average daily participants at full operating capacity in FY 2016, at an average contract cost of $5.16 per day.

- **Enhance Human Smuggling and Trafficking Investigations** ....$25.6 M (28 FTE)
  In FY 2016, HSI will expand current efforts to curb the high levels of human smuggling in the Southwest Border. HSI will hire 56 agents, intelligence specialist and investigative support staff, as well as put funds toward the purchase of information and evidence expenses, electronic surveillance equipment, analytical support, court-ordered communications intercepts (Title III wiretaps), expansion of Transnational Criminal Investigative Units (TCIU) and classified connectivity at the National Targeting Center Human Smuggling Cell.

- **Other HSI Domestic Investigations** ....$78.9M (135 FTE)
  This funding will be used to increase Domestic Investigative capacity. HSI will hire 201 Special Agents and 69 associated investigative and operational support personnel, as well as increase general expense levels needed to support domestic investigative operations such as costs for informants, undercover, and Title III operations.

- **Unaccompanied Children (UC) Contingency Funding** ....$27.6M (0 FTE)
  This funding will be available in increments of $6.9 million, if necessary, for costs associated with the transportation of more than 58,000 UC, and up to a maximum of 104,000 UC. The budget scores a total of $2.588 million of the $27.6 million that is potentially available to the Transportation and Removal Programs PPA based on calculated probabilities of incremental thresholds of UC apprehensions above 58,000 being met in FY 2016.

- **Internal Cyber Remediation** ....$13.3M (0 FTE)
  This request provides new security capabilities and enhances aging foundational security infrastructure capabilities. The remediation will focus on security enhancements needed to securely operate mission essential systems or those that have high" Federal Information Processing Standard" (FIPS) ratings. The funds will address vulnerabilities related to audit log management, security configuration management, disaster recovery, web application testing, and strong authentication capabilities.

- **TECS Modernization Project** ....$21.5M (0 FTE)
  The TECS Modernization solution will be the only system to provide case management functionality specific to the ICE mission once CBP discontinues its use of the legacy TECS system. The improved an update case management system will enable users to: acquire and manage law enforcement and criminal justice information on subjects of interest (i.e., people, organizations, etc.) in association with investigations, legal proceedings, and intelligence efforts; share law enforcement information with federal, state, local, tribal, and international law enforcement agencies; support the management of investigative and intelligence activities and assess the strategic and tactical immigration and customs law

enforcement environment. The priority of ICE TECS Modernization program is to reach Full Operating Capability (FOC) by the end FY 2017.

- **Consolidated ICE Financial Solutions (CIFS)** .... **$5M (0 FTE)**
  This initiative will allow ICE to make progress toward replacing the legacy core financial system that it owns and operates by acquiring financial management services from a Shared Service Provider (SSP). The SSP ICE selects will host and operate the core financial system for ICE and its customers. The requested increase will enable ICE's PMO to oversee efforts associated with the transition to the SSP(s). ICE will also support a solution for storing all financial management transaction data for ICE and DHS customer components in a non-proprietary repository to support reporting and migration. During FY 2016, ICE will support customer component migrations to an SSP, while preparing for its own migration anticipated in FY 2017 and FY 2018.

- **ICE Operational Data Store Initiative (IODS)** .... **$6.5M (0 FTE)**
  IODS is a new initiative that will provide integration of search, analysis and reporting tools. Currently data is spread out in disparate IT systems and data stores, which hinders ICE's ability to obtain and analyze the high-quality data it needs from across the agency to: support strategic and other management-level decisions in areas such as budgeting, resource allocation, and enforcement prioritization; satisfy internal and external reporting requirements; and identify leads, associations, and trends in support of law enforcement investigations and intelligence activities.

- **ICE Technical Refresh** .... **$22M (0 FTE)**
  The technical refresh funding will allow ICE to replace 140 network switches, 5,400 workstations, 140 file and print servers, refresh the Security Information and Event Management (SIEM) system, as well as procure two Intrusion Prevention System (IPS) sensors. ICE last received Atlas Program technical refresh funds in FY 2011. Systems that have not been refreshed in the last three to five years require complete replacement. The current SIEM is nearing end of life and replacing it with a new robust system will address 80 percent of the Security Operation Center's (SOC) priority technical requirements.

- **ICE Tactical Communication Program (TACCOM)** .... **$18.5M (0 FTE)**
  ICE's TACCOM technology foundation maximizes workforce productivity by providing expanded coverage and improved mobile command and control, and improves information sharing between ICE and U.S. Customs and Border Protection (CBP). The Program is charged with delivering TACCOM products and services that provide 24x7x365 systems availability that enable ICE and the Department of Homeland Security (DHS) to achieve their missions. The funding requested will be used to upgrade infrastructure nationwide including GPS technology, upgrade the Core/Hub, and fund Thin Client.

TRANSPORTATION SECURITY ADMINISTRATION

Description:

The *Aviation and Transportation Security Act* established the Transportation Security Administration (TSA) to provide security for the Nation's transportation system. TSA is an agency of more than 50,000 FTE, with approximately $7.3 billion in discretionary and mandatory budget authority, substantial regulatory authority, and a nationwide presence. As an intelligence driven counter-terrorism agency, TSA employs risk-based security principles to provide the most effective transportation security in the most efficient way.

Responsibilities:

The Nation's transportation systems are inherently "open" environments. TSA's mission is to protect the Nation's transportation systems, including aviation, mass transit, rail, highway, and pipeline, to ensure freedom of movement for people and commerce.

U.S. transportation systems accommodate: approximately 660 million domestic and international aviation passengers per year; 751 million passengers traveling on buses each year; more than 10 billion passenger trips on mass transit per year; 24 million students daily on school buses traveling more than 4 million miles annually; nearly 800,000 shipments of hazardous materials transported every day (95 percent by truck); more than 140,000 miles of railroad track; 3.9 million miles of roads; 604,000 bridges each spanning over 20 feet; 366 highway tunnels each over 100 meters in length; and nearly 2.6 million miles of pipeline.

TSA's mission performance and ability to achieve its shared goals and responsibilities is enhanced by its core values of integrity, innovation and team spirit.

TSA's specific responsibilities include the following:

- Ensuring effective and efficient screening of all air passengers, baggage, and cargo on passenger planes;

A Transportation Security Officer verifies a passenger's travel documents

- Deploying Federal Air Marshals internationally and domestically to detect, deter, and defeat hostile acts targeting air carriers, airports, passengers, and crew;

At a Glance

Senior Leadership:
Melvin Carraway, Acting Assistant Secretary

Established: 2001

Major Divisions: Security Operations, Security Policy and Industry Engagement, Law Enforcement/Federal Air Marshal Service, Security Technology, Information Technology, Intelligence and Analysis, and Transportation Security Support

Budget Request:	**$7,346,924,000**
Gross Discretionary:	$7,091,724,000
Mandatory, Fees & Trust Fund:	$255,200,000
Employees (FTE):	50,810

- Managing security risks of the surface transportation systems by working with public and private sector stakeholders, providing support and programmatic direction, and conducting on-site inspections to ensure the freedom of movement of people and commerce; and

- Developing and implementing more efficient, reliable, integrated, and cost-effective screening programs.

Service to the Public:

TSA is committed to the highest level of security for the United States across all modes of transportation. The Nation's economy depends upon implementation of effective, yet efficient transportation security measures. Public confidence in the security of the Nation's transportation systems ensures the continued success and growth of the industry. TSA engages the public in the security of the transportation system by encouraging them to report suspicious behavior. TSA also strives to provide excellent customer service to all travelers. TSA provides information to all travelers through its TSA Contact Center, Customer Service Managers in airports nationwide, the TSA website and blog, and Twitter and other social media outlets. Additionally, *TSA Cares* is a dedicated toll free number established to assist passengers or their loved ones with disabilities, medical conditions, or other special circumstances to prepare for the screening process.

TSA Social Media Outlets

Twitter: @TSA provides updates concerning national TSA related information.

TSA Blog: TSA Blog facilitates an ongoing dialogue on innovations in security, technology and the checkpoint screening process.

Instagram: The **@TSA Instagram account** features pictures of TSA and travel-related images.

APPS: My TSA (iTunes & Google play) provides passengers with 24/7 access to the most commonly requested TSA information on their mobile device.

Mobile Web Sites: MyTSA is the Mobile Web version of the MyTSA application.

Online Subscription Services: RSS and News Feeds (Really Simple Syndication) is an XML-based format for sharing and distributing Web content. Sign up to receive notifications for updates and newly posted items such as press releases or new content posted to tsa.gov.

YouTube: Transportation Security Administration Here you will find videos that support the agency's mission to protect the Nation's transportation systems to ensure freedom of movement for people and commerce.

FY 2014 Accomplishments:

- Screened approximately 660 million passengers, an estimated 1.6 billion carry-on bags at checkpoints and more than 440 million checked bags, preventing approximately 111,000 dangerous prohibited items including explosives, flammables/irritants, and 2,300 firearms from being carried onto planes.

- Increased the percent of passengers receiving expedited screening from a monthly average of 9.5% in September 2013 to 44.3% a year later. On August 12, 2014, TSA reached a nationwide high of 48.5% of all passengers receiving expedited screening.

- Increased TSA Pre✓® in FY14 from 40 airports to 119 airports and from 53 lanes to more than 450 full-time and part-time lanes; and enrolled 591,095 applicants in the TSA Pre✓® Application Program across 313 enrollment centers.

- Improved equipment capabilities nationwide including the deployment of 1,400 boarding pass scanners, the configuration of AT-2 X-rays, and the continued testing of Credential Authentication Technology for future use at the checkpoint.

- Procured 96 Explosive Detection System (EDS) units, most of which will be used to recapitalize the aging EDS fleet.

- Awarded three Screening Partnership Program (SPP) contracts which included five new airports to the program: four in Western Montana, the Orlando-Sanford airport in Florida, along with Roswell, New Mexico, an existing SPP airport.

- The Known Crewmember Program provided expedited screening for over 280,000 pilots and flight attendants each week at 55 U.S. airports, an average of over 40,000 per day.

- Through Secure Flight, TSA pre-screened an average of 6 million passengers daily, which included recurrent Watchlist matching.

- Processed over 447,318 Transportation Worker Identification Credential (TWIC) applicants, over 157,371 Extended Expiration Date requests, and expanded enrollment services to include both TWIC and Hazardous Materials Endorsement at all enrollment sites.

- The DHS Traveler Redress Inquiry Program reduced the processing time of cases by 40 percent, from 111 days to 66 days.

- Provided Federal Air Marshal Service (FAMS) coverage of highest priority flights in accordance with FAMS risk-based Concept of Operations.

- Conducted 16,849 Visible Intermodal Prevention and Response (VIPR) operations, 52% in the aviation and 48% in the surface environments to detect and deter terrorist activities.

- Trained 111 new canine teams: 79 Explosive Detection Canines and 32 Passenger Screening Canines.

- Completed over 1,054 airport inspections, 17,894 aircraft operator inspections, and 2,959 foreign air carrier inspections to ensure compliance with rules and regulations.

BUDGET REQUEST

Dollars in Thousands

	FY 2014 Revised Enacted [1]		FY 2015 President's Budget [2]		FY 2016 Request		FY 2016 +/- FY 2015	
	FTE	$000	FTE	$000	FTE	$000	FTE	$000
Aviation Security	49,427	4,937,705	49,203	5,683,304	47,367	5,614,766	(1,836)	(68,538)
Surface Transportation Security	624	108,618	860	127,637	818	123,828	(42)	(3,809)
Intelligence and Vetting [formerly Transportation Threat Assessment and Credentialing]	438	332,328	736	307,131	784	421,651	45	114,520
Transportation Security Support	1,790	962,061	1750	932,026	1,826	931,479	76	(547)
Federal Air Marshals	-	824,627	-		-	-	-	
Gross Discretionary	**52,279**	**7,165,339**	**52,549**	**7,050,098**	**50,795**	**7,091,724**	**(1,757)**	**41,626**
Mandatory, Fees, & Trust Fund	6	255,178	6	255,000	15	255,200	9	200
Total Budget Authority	**52,285**	**7,420,517**	**52,555**	**7,305,098**	**50,810**	**7,346,924**	**(1,745)**	**41,826**
Less prior year Rescissions		(59,209)						
Total	**52,285**	**7,361,308**	**52,555**	**7,305,098**	**50,810**	**7,346,924**	**(1,745)**	**41,826**

[1] FY 2014 Revised Enacted funding includes transfers which occurred in FY 2014. The FTE and fee funds represent actual FTE used and fees collected respectively.

[2] The FY 2015 President's Budget proposes to realign funding for the FAMS under the Aviation Security appropriation. The Request also proposes to realign Intelligence funding from the Transportation Security Support appropriation to the Intelligence and Vetting (formerly known as Transportation Threat Assessment and Credentialing) appropriation.

Passenger proceeds through Expedited Screening

The FY 2016 President's Budget includes $7.3 billion for TSA, reflecting a total gross discretionary increase of approximately $42 million from FY 2015. The Budget enables TSA to maintain its steadfast focus on maturing into a high-performing counterterrorism organization that applies intelligence-driven, risk-based security (RBS) principles across all operations. TSA continues to operate under three strategic priorities of risk-based security, workforce engagement, and organizational efficiency to meet its mission of protecting the Nation's transportation systems to ensure freedom of movement of people and commerce. As such, the Budget directs available resources to mission-critical programs and focuses on RBS initiatives to improve transportation security.

The FY 2016 Budget provides $13.4 million in additional funding to support DHS's Watchlist Service initiative to provide a single gateway for the Terrorist Screening Database; additional TSA Academy Instructors to train TSA's smaller, more professional screener workforce; lifting a FAMS hiring freeze; and remediation effort to enhance cyber security and protect critical network infrastructure. The Budget also includes $129.7 million in savings from RBS and other efficiencies, as follows: $119 million in workforce savings due to RBS efficiencies in the aviation sector; $4.3 million in efficiencies from the VIPR and Transportation Security Inspector – Surface programs; and $6.4 million in savings resulting from the delay in the General Aviation Security Rulemaking.

FY 2016 Highlights:

- **DHS Watchlist Service** ....………..**$2.8M (0 FTE)**
  The FY 2016 Budget includes an increase of $2.8 million to support the DHS Watchlist Service (WLS). TSA uses the DHS WLS which provides a single gateway of Terrorist Screening Database data from the Terrorist Screening Center to DHS. The Department acts as a service provider and manages the feed of terrorist Watchlist data to Secure Flight and the Transportation Vetting System (TVS). The new funding will cover the implementation of technological and operational sustainment and maintenance for Secure Flight and TVS's use of the DHS WLS.

- **TSA Academy Instructors**.. **$2.5M (31 FTE)**
  In support of TSA's efforts towards professionalization of the screening officer workforce, the Budget includes an additional $2.5 Million and 31 FTE to expand its mission essential training at the TSA Academy located at FLETC in Glynco, GA. This proposed increase will expand the courses conducted at the TSA Academy to include more categories of employees and support follow-on training that will continue to build upon the foundation established through the first Academy training deliveries.

- **Federal Air Marshal Service**...................…...................................... **$5.2M (0 FTE)**
  The FAMS has been subject to a hiring freeze for several years. The FY 2016 Budget provides $5.2 million to allow TSA to bring in new personnel to carry out FAMS operations.

- **High Risk Internal Cybersecurity Remediation**... **$2.9M (0 FTE)**
  An increase of $2.9 million for DHS-wide internal cybersecurity remediation efforts is included in the FY 2016 Budget. DHS's goal is to remediate all known vulnerabilities in the most high-risk systems by FY 2017, thereby enhancing critical network infrastructure protection. The funding increase supports corrective actions specific to TSA's individual systems as part of the overall departmental plan.

FY 2016 Major Decreases:

- **Risk-Based Security Efficiencies** ....-**$119.0M (1,748 FTE)**
  The FY 2016 Budget includes a reduction of $119.0 million and 1,748 FTE related to workforce savings due to RBS efficiencies in the aviation sector. TSA employs a multi-layered, risk-based, intelligence-driven approach to its security and counter-terrorism mission and operations. Through RBS initiatives, TSA is focusing its resources and enhancing the effectiveness and efficiency of its operations. RBS initiatives resulted in savings to the following workforce areas:

  - *Screener Workforce: ($110.5M) (1,666 FTE)* – RBS methods have proven more efficient in moving people through the checkpoint than regular screening lanes and require fewer resources than a traditional screening lane. This reduction reflects TSA's goal to continue transitioning to a smaller, more skilled, professional workforce capable of meeting the evolving requirements of RBS operations while ensuring the efficient movement of the traveling public.

  - *Transportation Security Inspectors (TSI): ($6.5M) (64 FTE)* – TSA has analyzed inspection data as well as risk scores to drive and prioritize inspection activity, taking into account several factors, including the latest intelligence information. As a result, TSA can achieve savings in the TSI workforce without significantly impacting security.

  - *Transportation Security Specialist – Explosives: ($2.0M) (18 FTE)* – As TSA transitions to a smaller, more skilled, professional workforce capable of meeting the evolving requirements of RBS, TSA is able to reduce the number of TSS-Es without significant negative impacts to security responsiveness and training. The TSS-E Program will continue operating at over 100 of the Nation's largest airports.

- **Visible Intermodal Prevention and Response Teams**............................. -**$3.1M (23 FTE)**
  The FY 2016 Budget includes a reduction of $3.1 million and 23 FTE for the elimination of two VIPR teams. The reduction would result in a decrease of total VIPR teams from 33 to 31. These savings will coincide with the closure of the co-located FAMS field offices.

- **Transportation Security Inspectors – Surface**............................-**$1.2M (13 FTE)**
  TSA did an in-depth analysis of the nationwide current TSI staffing, focusing on (1) how much work must be done; (2) how much time inspections take; and, (3) risk factors. TSA determined that it could reduce its TSI-S staffing allocation through attrition and the consolidation of vacant positions without degrading TSA's performance of its regulatory compliance oversight responsibilities.

- **Secure Flight** ....-**$6.4M (0 FTE)**
  The Budget includes a reduction of $6.4 million in the Secure Flight PPA due to a delay in the General Aviation Security Rulemaking. The reduction of $6.4 million will postpone modifications to the Secure Flight system, processes and procedures until the General Aviation Security Rule is further in the approval process. These modifications will ultimately allow Secure Flight to vet the passengers on large general aviation aircraft against the No-Fly and Selectee lists.

FY 2016 Other Adjustments:

- **Fee Increases (Aviation Passenger Security Fee and Air Carrier Fee)**

Separately from the FY 2016 President's Budget, TSA plans to submit two fee proposals that would adjust the Aviation Passenger Security Fee beginning in FY 2016 and the Air Carrier Fee beginning in FY 2017. The passenger fee proposal adjusts the fee from $5.60 per one-way trip to $6.00 per one-way trip in FY 2016, and would generate an additional $194.6 million in collections, of which all of the additional funds would be deposited into the general fund for deficit reduction in FY 2016. Starting in FY 2017, additional fee collections would contribute to deficit reduction and also begin to provide discretionary offsets for aviation security. The air carrier proposal reinstates the fee, repealed in FY 2015, at the previous amount of $420 million beginning in FY 2017. These proposals will further align the cost of passenger security operations to the direct beneficiaries of this security service and provide TSA greater financial flexibility to satisfy aviation security costs.

U.S. COAST GUARD

Description:

Since 1790, the Coast Guard has safeguarded our Nation's maritime interests and natural resources on our rivers, in U.S. ports, on the high seas, and in the maritime domain around the world. The Coast Guard saves those in peril and protects our Nation's maritime transportation system, resources, and environment.

Responsibilities:

The Coast Guard is the principal Federal agency responsible for maritime safety, security, and environmental stewardship in U.S. ports and inland waterways, along the coasts, throughout the U.S. Exclusive Economic Zone, and on the high seas. As one of the five Armed Services of the United States, the Coast Guard is the only military branch within the Department of Homeland Security (DHS). Unlike the military services in the Department of Defense (DoD), the Coast Guard is also a law enforcement and regulatory agency with broad legal authorities.

Service to the Public:

At a Glance	
Senior Leadership:	
Admiral Paul F. Zukunft, Commandant	
Vice Admiral Peter V. Neffenger, Vice Commandant	
Established: 1790 (as the Revenue Cutter Service; named U.S. Coast Guard in 1915)	
Major Programs:	
Maritime Security Operations	
Maritime Law Enforcement	
Maritime Prevention	
Maritime Response	
Defense Operations	
Marine Transportation System Management	
Budget Request:	***$9,963,913,900***
Gross Discretionary:	*$8,140,094,900*
Mandatory, Fees	
& Trust Funds:	*$1,823,819,000*
Civilian (FTE):	*8,088*
Military (FTE):	*41,141*
Additional Personnel:	
Military Selected Reserve:	*7,000*
Auxiliary:	*32,235*

Staten Island, New York – Members of Coast Guard Sector New York raise the American flag during a 9/11 rememberance ceremony.

The Coast Guard is an adaptable, responsive, military force of maritime professionals whose legal authorities, capable assets, geographic diversity, and expansive partnerships provide a persistent presence in our Nation's inland waters, ports, coastal regions, and offshore areas of operations. The Coast Guard leads responses to maritime disasters and threats, promotes a safe and secure marine transportation system, works to prevent maritime incidents and potential acts of terrorism, and rescues those in distress. The Coast Guard regulates hazardous cargo transportation, holding responsible parties accountable for environmental damage and cleanup, protecting living marine and natural resources. The Coast Guard enforces laws and treaties and guards the maritime domain against illegal activity.

FY 2014 Accomplishments:

Maritime Security Operations

- Conducted 19,779 waterborne patrols near critical maritime infrastructure and security zones in American ports.
- Conducted 623 law enforcement and security boardings of high interest vessels designated as posing a greater-than-normal risk to the U.S.

The crew of Coast Guard Cutter BOUTWELL stands at attention among pallets of cocaine seized during a 90-day counter drug patrol in which they made six drug interdictions.

Maritime Law Enforcement

- Removed over 91.0 metric tons of cocaine and 49.2 metric tons of marijuana from the maritime domain; detained 344 suspected drug smugglers.
- Interdicted 3,587 undocumented migrants attempting to illegally enter the U.S.

Maritime Prevention

- Completed inspections on 25,393 containers finding 2,046 deficiencies that led to 822 cargo or container shipments being placed on hold until dangerous conditions were corrected.
- Conducted over 43,700 recreational vessel boardings, issued almost 11,000 citations, and visited 426 recreational boat manufacturers to provide education and ensure compliance with Federal regulations.

Maritime Response

- Responded to 17,508 Search and Rescue incidents, saving 3,443 lives and more than $48.2 million in property.
- Received report of and responded to 8,905 pollution reports.

Defense Operations

- Continued the deployment of six patrol boats and their support and command elements to U.S. Central Command (CENTCOM).
- Coast Guard Port Security Units (PSU) deployed to the Middle East with Naval Coastal Warfare Squadrons to support point defense and harbor security operations in Kuwait, and continued port security operations in Guantanamo Bay, Cuba, for harbor security and force protection.

Marine Transportation System Management

- Maintained over 49,000 aids and corrected over 7,600 discrepancies to fixed and floating aids, providing a 98.2% Aid Availability Rate to ensure the safe transit of $1.7 trillion worth of commerce over 25,000 miles of U.S. waterways.
- In partnership with the Canadian Coast Guard, facilitated the safe movement of 34 million tons of dry bulk (iron ore, coal, stone, and cement) and over 20 million barrels of liquid (gasoline, diesel, and heating oil) cargoes to U.S. ports during the Great Lakes ice season.

BUDGET REQUEST
Dollars in Thousands

Appropriation ($000)	FY 2014 Revised Enacted[1]		FY 2015 Pres. Budget		FY 2016 Pres. Budget		FY 2016 +/- FY 2015	
	FTE	$	FTE	$	FTE	$	FTE	$
Operating Expenses (OE)	46,400	6,782,607	48,116	6,750,733	47,812	6,821,503	(304)	70,770
Environmental Compliance and Restoration (EC&R)	25	13,164	24	13,214	24	13,269	---	55
Reserve Training (RT)	503	120,000	416	109,605	416	110,614	---	1,009
Acquisition, Construction, and Improvements (AC&I)	737	1,373,135	881	1,084,193	881	1,017,269	---	(66,924)
Alteration of Bridges	---	---	---	---	---	---	---	---
Research, Development, Test, and Evaluation (RDT&E)	94	19,200	96	17,947	96	18,135	---	188
Health Care Fund Contribution (HFC)	---	185,958	---	176,970	---	159,306	---	(17,664)
Sub-total (Discretionary Funding)[2]	**47,759**	**$8,494,064**	**49,533**	**$8,152,662**	**49,229**	**$8,140,095**	**(304)**	**($12,567)**
Retired Pay	---	1,460,000	---	1,443,896	---	1,605,422	---	161,526
Boating Safety	11	105,874	14	112,830	14	115,776	---	2,946
Maritime Oil Spill Program	---	186,225	---	101,000	---	101,000	---	--
Gift Fund	---	2,049	---	80	---	1,621	---	1,541
Sub-total (Mandatory Funding)	**11**	**$1,754,148**	**14**	**$1,657,806**	**14**	**$1,823,819**	**---**	**$166,013**
OSLTF Contribution	---	[45,000]	---	[45,000]	---	[45,000]	---	---
Transfer to ICE for UACs	---	[-29,000]						
Hurricane Sandy Supplemental Funding from AC&I to OE	---	[26,800]	---	---	---	---	---	---
Overseas Contingency Operations	805	227,000	---	---	---	---	---	---
FY 2013 § 505 Rescission	---	(-3,879)	---	---	---	---	---	---
Rescission of unobligated balances	---	(149,459)	---	---	---	---	---	---
Transfer to DHS for UAC Emergency Reprogramming	---	[-2,500]						
Sub-total (Transfers and Supplementals)	**805**	**$73,662**	**---**	**---**	**---**	**---**	**---**	**---**
TOTAL BUDGET AUTHORITY[2]	**48,575**	**$10,321,874**	**49,547**	**$9,810,468**	**49,243**	**$9,963,913**	**(304)**	**$153,445**

[1]Reflects reprogrammings/transfers, as applicable, and actual FTE.
[2]Small differences due to rounding of individual appropriations.

FY 2016 Budget Priorities

The Coast Guard's FY 2016 Budget preserves Coast Guard operations and continues recapitalization efforts for the cutters, boats, aircraft, systems and infrastructure. The Budget also efficiently allocates resources to optimize Coast Guard mission performance. The Coast Guard must continue meeting today's operational requirements while investing in future capability to best serve the Nation.

The Coast Guard's FY 2016 budget priorities:
1. Invest in the 21st Century Coast Guard;
2. Sustain Mission Excellence; and
3. Maximize Service to Nation

Invest in the 21st Century Coast Guard
Coast Guard mission demands continue to grow and evolve. The complexities and challenges facing the Nation require well-trained Coast Guard men and women with capable platforms providing the persistent presence necessary to conduct operations. Given the age and condition of existing assets, future mission success relies on continued recapitalization of Coast Guard boats, cutters, aircraft, systems and infrastructure.

In support of the DHS's strategic objectives, the FY 2016 Budget provides for the acquisition of six Fast Response Cutters, continues to invest in pre-acquisition activities for an affordable Offshore Patrol Cutter and funds vessel sustainment projects for two 140' WTGB Icebreaking Tugs and a 225' Seagoing Buoy Tender. The budget also continues sustainment and conversion work on legacy fixed and rotary wing aircraft, missionization of the C-27J aircraft received from the Air Force, and investment in Command, Control, Communications, Computers, Intelligence, Surveillance, and Reconnaissance (C4ISR) systems.

Sustain Mission Excellence
The FY 2016 budget ensures the Coast Guard can conduct today's highest priority operations in support of national objectives. Most importantly, it sustains the Coast Guard's workforce and supports proficiency, maximizing operational safety and effectiveness. In 2016, the Coast Guard will decommission two Coastal Patrol Boats (WPBs) that are being replaced by more capable Fast Response Cutters. The Coast Guard will also decommission three HC-130 aircraft and corresponding support personnel while accepting the delivery of new C-130J aircraft and C-27J aircraft. In all, the FY 2016 budget sustains the Coast Guard's highest priority operations with current operational assets and the necessary workforce.

Maximize Service to Nation
In best serving the Nation, the Coast Guard must meet evolving mission requirements stemming from national priorities and remain a trusted steward of public resources. The 2016 Budget sustains critical frontline operations by efficiently allocating resources across all mission programs. Coast Guard Operational Commanders will continue maintaining search and rescue coverage, protecting critical infrastructure, countering illicit threats from entering the United States, facilitating a safe Marine Transportation System (MTS) to minimize disruptions to the transit of maritime commerce, safeguarding the maritime environment and supporting foreign policy objectives and defense operations.

FY 2016 Highlights:

Invest in the 21st Century Coast Guard

- **Surface Assets** ....$533.9M (0 FTE)
  The budget provides $533.9 million for the following surface asset recapitalization and sustainment initiatives:

  o **National Security Cutter (NSC)** – Provides funding for the Structural Enhancement Drydock Availability (SEDA) for the NSC and Post Delivery Activities for the fifth through eighth NSCs, completing the recapitalization of the Coast Guard's High Endurance Cutter fleet. The acquisition of the NSC is vital to performing DHS missions in the far off-shore regions, including the harsh operating environment of the Pacific Ocean, Bering Sea, and Arctic;

  o **Fast Response Cutter (FRC)** – Provides funding to procure six FRCs. These assets replace the aging fleet of 110-foot patrol boats that provide the coastal capability to conduct Search and Rescue operations, enforce border security, interdict drugs, uphold immigration laws, prevent terrorism, and enhance resiliency to disasters;

  o **Offshore Patrol Cutter (OPC)** – Supports technical review and analysis of preliminary and contract design phase deliverables for the OPC project. The Administration's request includes a General Provision permitting a transfer to the OPC project if the program is ready to award the next phase of vessel acquisition in FY 2016. The OPC will replace the Medium Endurance Cutter classes that conduct missions on the high seas and coastal approaches;

  o **Polar Ice Breaker (WAGB)** – Continues pre-acquisition activities for a new polar icebreaker;

  o **Cutter Boats** – Continues funding for production of multi-mission cutter small boats that will be fielded on the Coast Guard's major cutter fleet beginning with the NSC;

  o **In-Service Vessel Sustainment** – Continues funding for sustainment projects on 140-foot ice breaking tugs (WTGB), 225-foot seagoing buoy tenders, the training Barque EAGLE (WIX), and initial sustainment activities for the 47-foot motor lifeboats (MLB);

  o **Survey and Design** – Continues funding for multi-year engineering and design work for multiple cutter classes in support of future sustainment and acquisition projects.

- **Air Assets** ....$200.0M (0 FTE)
  The budget provides $200.0 million for the following air asset recapitalization or enhancement initiatives:

  o **HC-144A** – Funds spare parts required to maintain the operational availability of the HC-144A Ocean Sentry aircraft;

- o **HC-27J** – Funds continued activities of the C-27J Asset Project Office (APO). The APO organizes logistics, training, maintenance support and ensures these newly acquired aircraft are ready for induction into the operational fleet. Funds aircraft regeneration, spares, initial training, mission system development, ground support equipment to stand up first operational unit;

- o **HH-65** – Continues modernization and sustainment of the Coast Guard's fleet of HH-65 helicopters, converting them to MH-65 Short Range Recovery (SRR) helicopters. The modernization effort includes reliability and sustainability improvements, where obsolete components are replaced with modernized sub-systems, including an integrated cockpit and sensor suite;

- o **HC-130J** – Funds initial spare parts required for stand up of the second operational HC-130J unit.

- • **Other Acquisition, Construction and Improvements Initiatives..........$65.1M (0 FTE)**
  The budget provides $65.1 million for other initiatives funded under the Acquisition, Construction and Improvements account, including the following equipment and services:

  - o **Program Oversight and Management** – Funds activities associated with the transition of the Coast Guard's assets from acquisition to operations, including delivery, provision of logistics, training and other services necessary to ensure seamless integration into the operational fleet;

  - o **Command, Control, Communications, Computers, Intelligence, Surveillance, and Reconnaissance (C4ISR)** – Provides design, development, upgrades and assistance on C4ISR hardware and software, creating a common operational picture and ensuring interoperability of all new and in-service assets;

  - o **CG-Logistics Information Management System** – Continues development and deployment of a unified logistics system for Coast Guard operational assets.

- • **Shore Units and Aids to Navigation (ATON) ....$101.4M (0 FTE)**
  The budget provides $101.4 million to recapitalize shore infrastructure for safe, functional, and modern facilities that support Coast Guard assets and personnel:

  - o **Specific Projects** – Pier improvements in Little Creek, VA to facilitate 210' WMEC homeport shift; renovation and restoration of electrical system at Air Station Barbers Point, HI; the first phase of the replacement of aging dry-dock facilities at the Coast Guard Yard; erosion control work at Station Siuslaw River, OR; construction of permanent facilities at Station Vallejo, CA;

  - o **ATON Infrastructure** – Construction and improvements to short-range aids and infrastructure to improve the safety of maritime transportation.

  - o **Major Acquisition System Infrastructure** – Modification and construction of facilities to support newly delivered acquisitions. Includes upgrades and construction for NSC homeports, Medium Range Surveillance aircraft operational and maintenance facilities, and engineering, feasibility, and environmental studies for future projects.

- **Personnel and Management** ....**$116.9M (881 FTE)**
  The budget provides $116.9 million for pay and benefits of the Coast Guard's acquisition workforce.

Sustain Mission Excellence

- **Operational Adjustments**
  - **Cyber Security Remediation** ....**$5.2M (0 FTE)**
    This increase reflects a portion of a DHS-wide plan to address identified vulnerabilities related to a component controlled system, and the Department will track remediation of these vulnerabilities commencing in FY 2015.

  - **Support Structure Review and Rebalancing** ....**-$2.5M (-18 FTE)**
    A thorough review of the Coast Guard's support delivery structure identified personnel reductions at various locations that can be taken with no direct operational impacts and a minimal loss of current service delivery;

  - **National Capital Region Footprint Consolidation** ....**-$3.0M (0 FTE)**
    Reduces the Coast Guard's physical footprint in the National Capital region through consolidation of personnel and offices into the Douglas A. Munro Coast Guard Headquarters building at St. Elizabeths;

  - **Professional Services Contract Reduction** ....**-$44.9M (0 FTE)**
    Reduces or scales professional services contracts and redirects savings to higher priorities;

  - **Manual Continuous Monitoring Reduction**...............................**-$1.2M (0 FTE)**
    Due to increased capabilities of the Continuous Diagnostics and Mitigation (CDM) program, the need for manual cyber security monitoring is reduced, and the Coast Guard is able to achieve savings with no loss of IT system security;

  - **Headquarters Directorate Reduction** ....**-$5.0M (0 FTE)**
    Reduces funding for the overhead costs of Coast Guard headquarters directorates through a focused effort to minimize duplicative spending on consumable supplies and materials.

- **Asset Decommissioning and Retirement**
  As the Coast Guard recapitalizes its cutter and aircraft fleets and brings new assets into service, the older assets that are being replaced will be decommissioned or retired.

  - **Patrol Boat (WPB)** ....**-$1.1 M (-14 FTE)**
    Decommissions two 110-ft WPB patrol boats. These assets will be replaced with FRCs in the Seventh Coast Guard District.

  - **HC-130 Aircraft Retirement** ....**-$11.7M (-53 FTE)**
    Eliminates funding and personnel associated with the retirement of three HC-130H

to the Air Force for transfer to the U.S. Forest Service as outlined in the FY 2014 National Defense Authorization Act. Newly acquired HC-130J and C-27J aircraft will provide increased operational reliability.

Maximize Service to the Nation

- **Operating and Maintenance Funds for New Assets**..........................**$89.9M (222 FTE)**
Provides funding for operations and maintenance of shore facilities, as well as cutters, boats, aircraft, and associated C4ISR subsystems delivered through acquisition efforts.

  - **Shore Facilities** – Funds operation and maintenance of shore facility projects scheduled for completion by FY 2016;

  - **Response Boat-Medium** – Funds operation, maintenance and support of 4 RB-Ms;

  - **FRC** – Funds operation and maintenance of FRCs #18-21 and provides funding for personnel to operate and maintain hulls #19-22, including the shore-side support personnel;

  - **NSC** – Funds personnel for NSC #6, and costs for shore side support personnel for NSCs #4-5 (to be homeported in Charleston, SC);

  - **C-27JA Aircraft** – Funds operations, maintenance, and personnel funding for the first four C-27J aircraft that will be assigned to Air Station Sacramento, CA.

- **Pay & Allowances**..**$80.8 (0 FTE)**
Maintains parity with DoD for military pay, allowances, and health care, and for civilian pay raise and retirement contributions. As a branch of the Armed Forces of the United States, the Coast Guard is subject to the provisions of the National Defense Authorization Act, which include pay and personnel benefits for the military workforce.

U.S. SECRET SERVICE

Description:

The United States Secret Service carries out a unique dual mission of protection and investigation. The Secret Service protects the President, Vice President, former Presidents and their spouses, foreign visiting heads of state and government, National Special Security Events (NSSEs), the White House, the Vice President's residence, and other designated buildings within the Washington, D.C. area. The Secret Service also investigates financial and cyber crimes to safeguard the Nation's financial infrastructure and payment systems thus preserving the integrity of the economy.

The vision of the Secret Service is to uphold the tradition of excellence in its protective and investigative mission through a dedicated, highly trained, diverse, partner-oriented workforce that employs progressive technology and promotes professionalism.

At a Glance

Senior Leadership:
Joseph P. Clancy

Established: 1865

Major Divisions: Office of Protective Operations, Office of Investigations, Office of Technical Development and Mission Support, Office of Strategic Intelligence and Information, Office of Professional Responsibility, Office of Human Resources and Training, Office of Administration, Office of Government and Public Affairs, Office of the Chief Counsel, and Office of the Director

Budget Request: $2,204,122,000

Employees (FTE): 6,647

Responsibilities:

The Secret Service is responsible for the protection of the President, Vice President, President-elect,

A member of the Uniformed Division Emergency Response Team stands post at the White House.

Vice President-elect, their immediate families, former Presidents and their spouses; visiting foreign heads of state or government; major presidential and vice presidential candidates and their immediate families; former Vice Presidents and their spouses for a limited period of time; and other individuals as designated by the President. The Secret Service also protects the White House Complex, the Vice President's residence, and foreign and diplomatic missions located in the Washington, D.C. metropolitan area. It also implements operational security plans for designated NSSEs.

Using state-of-the-art countermeasures, the Secret Service executes security operations that prevent, deter, mitigate, and decisively respond to a myriad of threats. The protective environment consists of Uniformed Division Officers and special agents assigned to protective details and is enhanced by specialized resources within the Secret Service, which include, for example:

- Airspace Security Branch,
- Counter Sniper Teams,

- Emergency Response Teams,
- Counter Assault Teams,
- Counter Surveillance Teams,
- Explosive Detection Canine Teams,
- Critical Systems Protection Teams,
- Hazardous Agent Mitigation and Medical Emergency Response Teams, and the Magnetometer Operations Unit.

As part of the Secret Service's core objective of preventing incidents before they occur, the Protective Intelligence and Assessment Division (PID), utilizes a multifaceted approach to support protective operations through information analysis, threat investigation, risk assessment, and protective intelligence sharing. Daily, PID integrates information received from concerned citizens, the U.S. military, the intelligence community, and State, local, and Federal law enforcement agencies to assess the threat environment.

The Secret Service relies on long-standing partnerships cultivated through its domestic and international field offices to successfully execute its protective responsibilities. While providing permanent protective details to the President, Vice President, their immediate families and former Presidents, the backbone of the Secret Service is its network of 42 domestic field offices, 60 Resident Offices and Resident Agency Offices, and 24 international Resident investigative offices. In addition to investigating financial crimes, cyber crime investigations, and protective intelligence cases, these offices provide the surge capacity needed to successfully carry out the Secret Service's protection mission.

Secret Service investigations continue to safeguard the financial systems of the United States. The agency has evolved from enforcing counterfeiting laws to conducting a wide range of financial and cyber crimes investigations in order to preserve the integrity of U.S. currency. The Secret Service is proactive in its approach to these crimes, integrating advanced technologies with partnerships across the public and private sectors that are cultivated through specialized task forces around the world. Computer experts, forensic specialists, investigative experts, and intelligence analysts provide rapid responses and critical information in support of financial analysis, infrastructure protection, and criminal investigations.

Service to the Public:

In addition to the direct benefit to the public of providing protection to our Nation's highest leaders and ensuring the continuity of our government, the Secret Service is responsible for planning, coordinating, and implementing comprehensive operational security measures for NSSEs. These events include widely attended public gatherings such as presidential inaugurations. At these events, the Secret Service's responsibilities extend to all attendees, including the general public.

Through its network of domestic and international

Special agents from the Criminal Investigative Division utilize a cell phone tracking program.

field offices, the Secret Service fosters robust partnerships with State, local, Federal, and foreign law enforcement agencies that are crucial to the success of the agency's integrated mission. Financial and cyber crime investigations are enhanced through an established international network of 38 Electronic Crimes Task Forces (ECTF) and 46 Financial Crimes Task Forces (FCTF). These task forces combine resources from the law enforcement community and the private sector, resulting in an organized effort to combat threats to the Nation's financial payment systems and critical infrastructures. The Secret Service's financial crimes investigations have prevented billions of dollars in losses to the American taxpayer over the years.

FY 2014 Accomplishments:

- Provided protection during 3,672 travel stops for domestic protectees and 2,512 travel stops for visiting foreign dignitaries.

- Provided protection for former presidents and spouses for 1,450 protective visits.

- Uniformed Division Officers completed 505 magnetometer/X-ray mission assignments and successfully screened more than 1,410,061 members of the public at 943 protective venues.

- Provided protection for 142 foreign heads of state/government and 76 spouses at the 69th United Nations General Assembly in New York, New York.

- Designed and implemented comprehensive security plans for the United States–Africa Leaders Summit in Washington, D.C. (NSSE) in August 2014.

- Safeguarded the currency of the United States by making 2,438 counterfeit-related arrests.

- Seized $58 million domestically and overseas prior to entering circulation.

- Suppressed more than 185 counterfeit manufacturing operations domestically.

- Prevented $3 billion in potential losses and made more than 1,000 cyber crime arrests.

- Continued support for the existing 22 mobile investigative teams that provide regional coverage and mission support throughout the United States.

- The Treasury Obligations Section continued to work with the Bureau of Engraving and Printing, Federal Reserve Banks, and the U.S. Treasury Department in the production and release of the newly designed $100 Federal Reserve Note.

- Completed 211 Critical System Protection advances in support of the Secret Service protective mission.

- Provided money laundering and mortgage fraud training courses for field investigators on the emerging fraud scams and methods that threaten the Nation's financial and payment systems infrastructure.

- Provided protection, through the Uniformed Division, for 548 foreign diplomatic missions located in the Washington, D.C. metropolitan area.

- Completed the initial development of the Bank Note Processing System for the Counterfeit Operations Section. This system automates the processing and categorization of counterfeit U.S. Currency, which reduces overall labor hours.

- Strategic high-profile cyber investigations resulted in the international arrests of high-level "King Pin" cyber criminals including the capture of Roman Seleznev, Ercan Findikoglu, and Sergey Vovnenko.

BUDGET REQUEST
Dollars in Thousands

	FY 2014 Revised Enacted		FY 2015 President's Budget		FY 2016 President's Budget		FY 2016 +/- FY 2015	
	FTE	$000	FTE	$000	FTE	$000	FTE	$000
Operating Expenses	6,572	$1,538,497	6,572	$1,585,970	6,647	$1,867,453	75	$281,483
AC&I		$51,775		$49,935		$71,669		$21,734
Gross Discretionary	**6,572**	**$1,590,272**	**6,572**	**$1,635,905**	**6,647**	**$1,939,122**	**75**	**$303,217**
Mandatory/DC Annuity		$255,000		$260,000		$265,000		$5,000
Less prior year Rescissions		($952)						
Total	**6,572**	**$1,844,320**	**6,572**	**$1,895,905**	**6,647**	**$2,204,122**	**75**	**$308,217**

FY 2016 Highlights:

- **2016 Presidential Campaign**... **$123.5M (0 FTE)**
The Secret Service is mandated by law (Title 18 U.S.C. § 3056) to provide protection and security for "Major Presidential and Vice Presidential candidates and, within 120 days of the general Presidential election, the spouses of such candidates." In addition, the Secret Service will provide security at major political conventions and debates. During presidential campaigns, the Secret Service experiences a significant increase in its protective workload as it provides protection for the designated candidates/nominees, in addition to its other protective responsibilities.

- **Former President Obama Protective Detail** .... **$25.7M (29 FTE)**
The Secret Service is mandated by law (Title 18 U.S.C § 3056) to provide protection to all former Presidents and their spouses for life. Consequently, the Secret Service is required to establish a permanent, post-presidency protective division for President Obama at the end of his term in office. The Obama Protective Division (OPD) must be fully staffed, trained, and positioned by January 20, 2017. The OPD will also be responsible for the protection of the former First Lady and at least one minor child.

- **Protective Mission Enhancements** .... **$86.7M (0 FTE)**
This funding will support security enhancements at the White House Complex pursuant to the recommendations of the United States Secret Service Protective Mission Panel.

NATIONAL PROTECTION AND PROGRAMS DIRECTORATE

Description:

The National Protection and Programs Directorate (NPPD) leads national efforts to strengthen the security and resilience of the Nation's critical infrastructure against terrorist attacks, cyber events, natural disasters, other large-scale incidents, and during national security special events. Secure and resilient infrastructure is essential for national security, economic vitality, and public health and safety. NPPD collaborates with the owners and operators of infrastructure to maintain near real-time situational awareness of both physical and cyber events and share information that may disrupt critical infrastructure. Through partnerships with Federal, State, local, tribal, territorial, international, and private-sector entities, NPPD identifies and enables mitigation and risk reduction to infrastructure and builds capacity to secure the Nation.

At a Glance	
Senior Leadership:	
Suzanne Spaulding, Under Secretary	
Established: 2007	
Major Divisions: Infrastructure Protection, Cybersecurity and Communications, Cyber and Infrastructure Analysis, Biometric Identity Management, Federal Protective Service	
Budget Request:	**$3,102,862,000**
Net Discretionary	*$1,659,413,000*
Collections:	*$1,443,449,000*
Employees (FTE):	*3,527*

Responsibilities:

NPPD works with infrastructure owners and operators, along with others in the private sector; Federal, State, local, territorial, and tribal officials; and international partners to ensure timely information, analysis, and assessments in order to maintain and provide situational awareness, increase resilience, and understand and mitigate risk through its field force and headquarters components. Through established partnerships, NPPD leads the national unity of effort for infrastructure security and resilience and builds capacity of partners across the Nation through activities like bombing prevention, technical assistance, training, analysis, and assessments. NPPD also directly protects Federal infrastructure against both physical and cyber threats and responds to incidents which threaten infrastructure at the local level.

NPPD informs decision-makers on potential impacts from all hazards through comprehensive consequence analysis during both steady-state and crisis action. NPPD utilizes integrated analysis and modeling capabilities to understand cyber and physical risk and assist with prioritization of infrastructure to ensure resources are focused to maximize effectiveness. This capability also enables NPPD to maintain and provide situational awareness to public and private sector partners.

NPPD reduces cyber and physical risks to critical infrastructure through collaboration with various partners via frameworks established in the National Infrastructure Protection Plan. Through its Protective Security Advisor and Cyber Security Advisor programs, NPPD works with partners to conduct voluntary critical infrastructure and cybersecurity assessments. These assessments allow partners to better understand their physical and cyber security resilience and vulnerabilities and provide recommendations for how they can improve resilience and mitigate vulnerabilities.

NPPD programs create a safer and more secure cyber environment and promote cybersecurity knowledge and innovation by: enabling Federal departments and agencies to address cybersecurity challenges with technology, analysis, and best practices; partnering with the private sector, military, and intelligence communities to mitigate vulnerabilities and threats to information technology assets; and facilitating collaboration and partnerships on cyber issues with public and private sector partners.

OBIM's BSC processed more than 631,000 10-Print verifications and completed over 239,000 urgent fingerprint verifications during FY 2014.

NPPD provides direct protection and conducts incident response activities to support the protection of cyber networks and Federal facilities and regulates high-risk chemical facilities. NPPD secures and protects the buildings, grounds, and property owned or occupied by the Federal Government, as well as the people on those properties, by conducting Facility Security Assessments, recommending appropriate countermeasures, overseeing a large contract Protective Security Officer workforce, and exercising law enforcement authorities.

NPPD is responsible for ensuring effective telecommunications for government users in national emergencies and for establishing policies and promoting solutions for interoperable emergency communications at the Federal, State, and local levels used on a daily basis across the country. As the Sector Specific Agency for Communications and for Emergency Services, NPPD protects and strengthens the security, reliability, survivability, and interoperability of the Nation's communications capabilities at the Federal, State, local, tribal, and territorial levels.

NPPD provides enterprise-level biometric identity management services to customers across DHS, at other Federal agencies, in State and local law enforcement, and to foreign partners through storing biometric identities, recurrent matching against derogatory information, and providing other biometric expertise and services. These services broaden the scope of information available and lead to identifying tens of thousands of known or suspected terrorist and Watchlist matches every year in support of efforts to protect critical infrastructure and the American public.

Service to the Public:

NPPD protects critical infrastructure to ensure that those assets, systems, and networks that underpin American society, including essential government missions, public services, and economic functions, are sustained in a way that permits safe and secure use during steady-state and all-hazards situations. NPPD coordinates security and resilience efforts using trusted partnerships with Federal partners, private sector owners and operators, State and local government agencies, and others. NPPD provides the unifying framework for all of infrastructure and enables infrastructure owners and operators to collaborate and understand the risk associated with infrastructure in order to protect the Nation. In executing its mission, NPPD balances security concerns with privacy and safeguarding of civil liberties. For example, during the past year, NPPD published or updated six Privacy Impact Assessments (PIAs) in order to evaluate the privacy impacts of the systems and information sharing capabilities associated with NPPD systems. Among the newly published PIAs were assessments of the National Cybersecurity Protection System (NCPS), ECS, and E3A. NPPD also continued to safeguard sensitive private sector business information through its Protected Critical Infrastructure Information program, ensuring that critical infrastructure vulnerability information voluntarily submitted to the Department in order to formulate mitigation strategies is protected.

FY 2014 Accomplishments:

- Conducted more than 200 classified and unclassified meetings with critical infrastructure partners to share actionable information and recommend preventative measures, identify and promulgate best practices, and determine requirements for risk mitigation. Examples include awareness campaigns conducted jointly with the FBI to share information on countermeasures with mall owners in the U.S. and an electricity substation security campaign in 12 cities related to the attack on the Metcalf, CA substation, which demonstrated the interdependencies between cyber and physical infrastructure.

- Conducted 10 Regional Resiliency Assessment Program (RRAP) projects including the first climate change RRAP located in Maine, and the first cyber focused RRAP in Charlotte, NC to enhance resilience and address security gaps within those geographic regions.

- Continued to build trusted relationships across government and private sector. Received approximately 56,000 cyber incident reports from Federal and critical infrastructure stakeholders. Improved upon ability to provide rapid and comprehensive operational support to partners through deployment of world-class cyber incident response teams. Conducted 17 on-site responses to cyber incidents and identified over 64,000 cybersecurity vulnerabilities through scans and vulnerability assessments.

- Deployed EINSTEIN 3 Accelerated (E3A) capabilities that have the capacity to protect 500,000 Federal users from malicious e-mail attacks (such as e-mail-initiated spear phishing campaigns) or malware installed on .gov networks from communicating with external entities attempting to control that malware.

- Delivered Continuous Diagnostics and Mitigation tools and sensors to 21 Federal civilian departments and agencies (approximately 75-percent of the Federal Executive Branch seats), which allows them to determine whether devices connected to federal networks are vulnerable to threats.

- Under the Chemical Facility Anti-Terrorism Standards program, successfully authorized nearly 1,500 site security plans or alternative security programs for high-risk chemical facilities and conducted more than 1,000 Authorization Inspections, resulting in approval of approximately 885 SSPs/ASPs. Conducted Compliance Inspections at more than 50 facilities.

- In response to a series of high profile attacks targeting government facilities and officials overseas, NPPD initiated surges of law enforcement and security experts at Federal government buildings in several cities. These operations enhanced the immediate security of 189 facilities and over 87,000 tenants, and improved communications interoperability of local, state and federal law enforcement. NPPD also surged personnel and assets in order to secure Federal property, employees and the visiting public during high profile incidents and terrorist trials, such as court appearances related to the Boston Marathon bombing

- NPPD screening operations interdicted and confiscated more than 636,000 prohibited and illegal items such as firearms, knives, and drug paraphernalia at Federal facilities to render those properties secure.

- Processed over 88 million total transactions with more than 2.7 million Watchlist identifications, including 350,754 Known Suspected Terrorist matches identified. Completed more than 4.4 million latent fingerprint comparisons and provided 2,318 identifications. Completed nearly 3,800 manual fingerprint searches of IDENT supporting law enforcement agency requests, including unknown deceased cases, criminal cases, and mass casualty incidents.

- Completed over 250 communications interoperability technical assistance engagements in 54 States and territories, including broadband consultation preparation workshops and 26 communications interoperability workshops; and supported States and territories in developing statewide Interoperable Emergency Communications Guides.

BUDGET REQUEST
Dollars in Thousands

	FY 2014 Revised Enacted		FY 2015 President's Budget		FY 2016 President's Budget		FY 2016 +/- FY 2015	
	FTE	$000	FTE	$000	FTE	$000	FTE	$000
Management and Administration	305	56,069	358	65,910	367	64,191	9	(1,719)
Infrastructure Protection and Information Security	1,373	1,184,750	1,544	1,197,566	1,606	1,311,689	62	114,123
Office of Biometric Identity Management	207	226,988	190	251,584	168	283,533	(22)	31,949
Federal Protective Service	1,371	1,342,606	1,371	1,342,606	1,386	1,443,449	15	100,843
Gross Discretionary	**3,256**	**2,810,413**	**3,463**	**2,857,666**	**3,527**	**3,102,862**	**64**	**245,196**
Offsetting Collections	(1,371)	(1,342,606)	(1,371)	(1,342,606)	(1,386)	(1,443,449)	(15)	(100,843)
Total Budget Authority (Net Discretionary)	**1,885**	**1,467,807**	**2,092**	**1,515,060**	**2,141**	**1,659,413**	**49**	**144,358**
Less prior year Rescissions		(239)						
Total	1,885	1,467,568	2,092	1,515,060	2,141	1,659,413	49	144,353

FY 2016 Highlights:

- **Develop Situational Awareness & Infrastructure Analysis ....$10.4M (19 FTE)**
  Funds enhancements in cybersecurity situational awareness and information sharing. This includes Integrated Analysis Cell, STIX/TAXII, Media & Collective Analysis, National Cybersecurity Technical Services teams, and ensures that standards are integrated into the architecture for collected data, enabling NPPD to better integrate cyber and physical data.

- **Strengthen Partnerships and Foster Capacity Building ....…....…...$36.2M (9 FTE)**
  Funds will strengthen partnerships and foster capacity building, expands the Office of Bombing Prevention, C3 Voluntary Program, and Enhanced Cybersecurity Services.

- **Improve the Protection of Infrastructure: Ammonium Nitrate Security........ $15.7M (12 FTE)**
  Funds the Ammonium Nitrate Security Program to support implementation of a regulatory program to protect the public from future misuse of ammonium nitrate in an act of terrorism.

- **National Cybersecurity Protection System (NCPS) Information Sharing........$67.8M (0 FTE)**
  Enables complete deployments of foundational infrastructure capabilities for information sharing, and complete development of information sharing applications. Additional funding will support planned design, development, and deployment of a COOP Information Sharing Collaboration Environment (ISCE), the Top Secret environment of the ISCE, and the Cross Domain Solution (CDS) between the Secret and Top Secret environments.

- **NCPS Intrusion Prevention .... S28.1M (9 FTE)**
  Provides countermeasures beyond email and Domain Name System at four Internet Service Providers through NCPS E3A. These new capabilities will leverage machine learning processing output through various pre-defined business rules and correlation mechanisms with enough certainty to automatically task intrusion prevention systems to block the suspicious activity, changing the time between attack occurrence, detection, and prevention from months to minutes.

- **Continuous Diagnostics & Mitigation Increments 1 and2 ....$86.5M (0 FTE)**
  Funds Increments 1 and 2 of the Continuous Diagnostics & Mitigation program, which provides the necessary software and services that will allow DHS and Federal agencies to continuously monitor users and their privileges on Federal networks.

- **Next Generation Networks (NGN) Increment 2 ....$78.6M (0 FTE)**
  Provides support to maintain the number of wireless carriers deploying Priority Telecommunications Services, enabling the solution to maintain the same degree of coverage across the United States regardless of the underlying technology. These funds will transition the Wireless Priority Services infrastructure to internet-based technologies through implementation of Phase 1, Increment 2 of the NGN Priority Services program.

- **Replacement Biometric System ....$65.8M (0 FTE)**
  Supports OBIM's initial increment of a four increment phased approach to transform its biometric capabilities and services from the legacy IDENT system to a Replacement Biometric System. This funding will provide for the planning and implementation, acquisition, and operations and maintenance of Increment 1. Key benefits of the replacement system will be Operations and Maintenance cost avoidance, improved detection and multi-modal capabilities, more efficient transaction processing, and an improved ability to scale the system to meet stakeholder/user requirements.

OFFICE OF HEALTH AFFAIRS

Description:

OHA's mission is to advise, promote, integrate, and enable a safe and secure workforce and Nation in pursuit of national health security. The Office of Health Affairs (OHA) achieves this by enhancing the health and wellness of the DHS workforce, and by protecting the Nation from the health impacts of incidents, including biological and chemical events.

Responsibilities:

OHA's responsibilities include serving as the principal advisor to the Secretary, Federal Emergency Management Agency (FEMA) Administrator, and other DHS officials and components on medical and health issues. In addition, OHA supports DHS chemical and biological defense activities, including pandemic preparedness; provides medical and health expertise for DHS preparedness, response, and resilience efforts; enhances national and DHS medical first responder capabilities; and supports the Department's occupational health and operational medicine activities, including providing policies and guidance to other DHS components and Federal agencies. Through its Food, Agriculture, and Veterinary Defense Program, OHA provides oversight and management of DHS's implementation of Homeland Security Presidential Directive (HSPD)-9 Defense of United States Agriculture and Food.

> *At a Glance*
>
> *Senior Leadership:*
>
> *Kathryn Brinsfield MD, MPH*
> *Acting Assistant Secretary for Health Affairs and Chief Medical Officer*
>
> *Established: 2007*
>
> *Major Divisions: Health Threats Resilience; Workforce Health & Medical Support; Management & Administration*
>
> ***Budget Request: $124,069,000***
>
> *Employees (FTE): 96*

Service to the Public:

OHA supports the Department's mission in the following ways:

Serves as Principal Medical Advisor to DHS Leadership

OHA ensures that the Department's leaders have relevant, evidence-based public health and medical information and recommendations to guide policy decisions and response actions.

Coordinates Health Security Activities

OHA is the Department's lead on interagency efforts involving health and medical issues. OHA helps to build resilience by working with DHS components and offices to provide appropriate information, resources, and guidance to help State and local communities prepare for and respond to health threats.

Supports DHS Biodefense and Detection Programs

OHA manages the Department's biological detection and surveillance programs. OHA helps to improve national resilience by informing biodefense policies, planning and exercises, providing guidance to responders and other

BioWatch uses a network of portable sampling units (PSUs) to collect air samples for analysis for the presence of biological threat agents. At the National BioWatch Stakeholders' Workshop, friendly competition reinforces training and proper procedures.

stakeholders on protective actions, and engaging interagency partners on biodefense policy and capability development efforts. OHA integrates, analyzes, and shares the Nation's biosurveillance information across Federal, State, and local entities and the private sector, to contribute to early warning and shared situational awareness of potential biological events. This information analysis and sharing informs decision-makers and improves the efficiency and efficacy of any necessary response and recovery efforts.

Improves the Health of the DHS Workforce and Provides Medical Support

National Biosurveillance Integration Center (NBIC) staff demonstrates the NBIC's capabilities to visiting senior Federal officials and Congressional representatives.

DHS has one of the largest operational workforces in the Federal Government, and the health and safety of this workforce continues to be a priority of DHS leadership. OHA develops strategy, policy, standards, and metrics for the health and medical aspects of the Department's occupational health and safety activities. It provides medical quality management subject matter experts who ensure that health care service standards are consistently and appropriately applied across the Department. In addition, OHA works to ensure that occupational health and medicine principles are incorporated into traditional occupational safety, health, and wellness programs throughout DHS. OHA procures, manages, and distributes medical countermeasures to the entire DHS workforce, and to those under DHS care and custody. OHA also embeds experienced health care physicians in DHS operational Components to provide subject matter expertise and medical advice in support of Component activities.

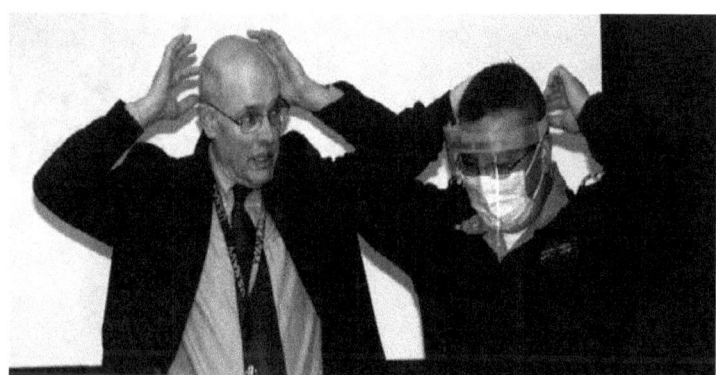

Dr. Michael Montopoli, Occupational Medicine Physician, and CAPT Joselito Ignacio, Industrial Hygienist, demonstrate the use of personal protective equipment (PPE) to DHS employees. Several subject matter experts from OHA, including Dr. Montopoli, deployed to airports selected for enhanced Ebola screening in October 2014 to train U.S. Customs and Border Protection officers on proper use and removal of PPE.

Improves Chemical Defense

OHA's Chemical Defense Program (CDP) provides health and medical expertise related to chemical preparedness, detection, response, and resilience. OHA provides subject matter expertise on medical toxicology, industrial hygiene, and responder workforce protection related to chemical threats and works directly with communities to help them understand their capabilities and limitations. The program helps communities integrate threat-based risk assessments and detection capabilities to improve community preparedness.

Enhance DHS and National Medical First Responders Capabilities

OHA serves as the primary DHS office that supports the external and internal medical first responder communities. OHA plays a key role in integrating the emergency medical services (EMS) community into Federal, State, local, territorial, and tribal disaster preparedness and resilience activities. It builds and leverages collaborative working relationships between DHS and major EMS national associations to address gaps, enhance efficiency, and develop medical first responder and EMS best practices for use in disaster planning, preparedness, response, and recovery. OHA supports the more than 3,500 DHS personnel with medical responsibilities by developing health guidance, socializing policies, and sharing best practices. OHA provides medical oversight of the internal health care and EMS performed by DHS operating Components, including oversight and verification of credentials for the Department's medical providers. In addition, OHA provides detailed guidance for external medical first responders, and is working closely with other Federal agencies and the National Security Council to develop and distribute medical guidance for first responders on improving survivability of improvised explosive device (IED) and active shooter incidents.

FY 2014 Accomplishments:

OHA Support to DHS Southwest Border and Emerging Infectious Disease Response Operations

- Provided, through the National Biosurveillance Integration Center (NBIC), enhanced situational awareness for multiple high priority events including the Middle East Respiratory Syndrome Coronavirus, China Avian Influenza virus A, and Ebola.

- Worked with CBP and other federal agencies to improve and strengthen the targeting, detection, and interception of Ebola contaminated "bushmeat" prior to its entry into the US.

- Provided medical policy expertise and support to the interagency and DHS in development of the unaccompanied alien children medical clearance annex (Annex D. Medical Clarence to the Unified Coordination Group Plan for Unaccompanied Children Surge), the Rio Grande Valley Communicable Disease Contingency Plan, and revision of the Medical Annex Q of the Mass Migration Plan.

- Credentialed 52 licensed healthcare providers to support the Department's response to the surge in unaccompanied alien children at the southwest border.

Health Threats Resilience

- Held a National BioWatch Stakeholders' Workshop attracting between 450-500 participants from federal, state and local public health, emergency management and risk communication organizations. The workshop focused on sharing lessons in order to improve existing plans and develop new strategies.

- Completed Indoor Guidance and updated Outdoor Guidance providing jurisdictions with information necessary to prepare for and to guide activities following a BioWatch Actionable Result (BAR); instituted near real-time tracking of Field Operations; identified technology to be used to upgrade Laboratory Operations; completed an operational demonstration; and documented Polymerase Chain Reaction assay performance for Variola major (smallpox).

- Completed prototype tools that initially will allow NBIC analysts to more effectively and efficiently visualize, filter, and contextualize open source and social media information for early detection and situational awareness of biological events of national concern. When fully operational the tool will be available to Federal interagency partners.

- Conducted a Tabletop Exercise for the Maryland Transit Administration Demonstration Project and initiated four new demonstration projects in Houston, Boise, New Orleans, and Nassau County, which were designed to identify best practices and discover common challenges in response to large-scale chemical incidents.

- Published "Patient Decontamination in a Mass Chemical Exposure Incident: National Planning Guidance for Communities" guidelines, in partnership with the Department of Health and Human Services.

- Partnered with the National Association for States Departments of Agriculture to create a model state-level catastrophic food event plan in response to food borne illnesses, contamination, and shortages.

- Conducted a Food and Agriculture Tabletop Exercise for over 150 Federal, state, local, tribal and territorial stakeholders that informed the Region VII Food, Agriculture, and Veterinary Annex to the Region's All-Hazards Plan.

- Responded to requests for guidance and information related to public health collaboration with fusion centers from 20 states in Fiscal Year 2014 and processed Secret clearances for 52 state and local health officials.

Workforce Health & Medical Support

- Published the DHS Medical Liaison Officers program framework formalizing senior-level strategic medical subject matter expertise for DHS Components to coordinate, centralize, and standardize medical programmatic direction, enhance deployment readiness and preparedness, increase medical protection, and improve workforce health and wellness.

- Provided Senior Medical Advisors and Medical Liaison Officers to CBP, FEMA, TSA, and ICE.

- Fostered continued growth of DHS continuous quality improvement efforts. Medical Quality Management Branch (MQM) implemented Medical Quality Management on the Go initiative, which provides for regular face-to-face engagement with the DHS Components and distribution of the DHS Health Care Quality Committee Education and Training Newsletter.

- Led first responder stakeholder engagement with over 200 Federal, state, and local, EMS, fire, and law enforcement professionals in attendance, to aid in improving survivability in IED and active shooter incidents.

- Developed emergency medical care under fire education standards for the training of DHS agents and officers.

- Achieved cost avoidance of $19 million worth of medical countermeasures through the FDA/DoD Shelf–Life Extension Program.

- Formalized a "DHSTogether" senior-level council to provide strategic direction for the enhancement of employee resilience.

BUDGET REQUEST

Dollars in Thousands

	FY 2014 Revised Enacted		FY 2015 President's Budget		FY 2016 President's Budget		FY 2016 +/- FY 2015	
	FTE	$000	FTE	$000	FTE	$000	FTE	$000
BioWatch	-	85,277	-	84,651	-	83,278	-	(1,373)
National Biosurveillance Integration Center	-	10,000	-	8,000	-	8,000	-	0
Planning and Coordination	-	4,995	-	4,995	-	4,957	-	(38)
Chemical Defense Program	-	824	-	824	-	824	-	0
Salaries and Expenses	99	25,667	99	27,297	96	27,010	(3)	(287)
Net Discretionary	**99**	**126,763**	**99**	**125,767**	**96**	**124,069**	**(3)**	**(1,698)**
Gross Discretionary	**99**	**126,763**	**99**	**125,767**	**96**	**124,069**	**(3)**	**(1,698)**
Total Budget Authority	**99**	**126,763**	**99**	**125,767**	**96**	**124,069**	**(3)**	**(1,698)**
Less prior year Rescissions	-	(91)	-	-	-	-	-	-
Total	**99**	**126,672**	**99**	**125,767**	**96**	**124,069**	**(3)**	**(1,698)**

FY 2016 Highlights:

- **BioWatch**..-$1.4M (FTE)
  The activities of the BioWatch program ensure the Department's capability to provide preparedness, detection, and information sharing with Federal, State, and local partners related to biological threat agent incidents, whether naturally occurring, accidental, or deliberately caused by an adversary. The requested funding for BioWatch will enable the continuation of current operations in all jurisdictions where the BioWatch program is presently deployed and operating.

- **Planning and Coordination (P&C)**..-$38K (0 FTE)
  The programs within Planning and Coordination support a suite of activities that bolster health security preparedness and resilience, both within DHS and throughout the Nation. This includes providing medical and health subject matter expertise to support the Department in achieving its mission. The WHMS portion of P&C is composed of Health and Medical Support, including Occupational and Operational Medicine. The HTR portion of P&C is composed of Health Security Integration, Planning and Exercise Support, State and Local Initiatives, and Food, Agriculture, and Veterinary Defense.

- **Salaries and Expenses** ....-$0.3M (3 FTE)
  The Assistant Secretary for Health Affairs and Chief Medical Officer leads a team of highly skilled professionals who provide expertise and specialized abilities that are essential to achieving OHA's mission. OHA's staff is composed of doctors, veterinarians, nurses, scientists, public health professionals, and other public servants recruited for their experience and skills.

FEDERAL EMERGENCY MANAGEMENT AGENCY

Description:

The mission of the Federal Emergency Management Agency (FEMA) is to support our citizens and first responders to ensure that, as a Nation, we work together to build, sustain, and improve our capability to prepare for, protect against, respond to, recover from, and mitigate all hazards.

In addition to its headquarters in Washington, D.C., FEMA has 10 permanent regional offices, three permanent area offices, and various temporary disaster-related sites that carry out the Agency's operations throughout the United States and its territories.

The FY 2016 President's Budget provides the resources to support FEMA's ability to work with its partners in strengthening the Nation's preparedness for and resilience to future disasters. The Budget reflects lessons learned from recent disasters as well as overall trends in disaster losses. The agency has

At a Glance	
Senior Leadership:	
W. Craig Fugate, Administrator	
Joseph Nimmich, Deputy Administrator	
Timothy Manning, Deputy Administrator for	
Protection and National Preparedness	
Established: 1979; transferred to DHS in 2003	
Major Components: Protection and National Preparedness, Response and Recovery, Federal Insurance and Mitigation Administration, Mission Support, United States Fire Administration, 10 Operational Regions	
Budget Request:	**$15,467,013,600**
Net Discretionary:	*$10,801,316,600*
Mandatory, Fees,	
& Trust Fund:	*$4,665,697,000*
Employees (FTE):	12,252
Disaster Relief Fund	*7,134*
Other Appropriations	*5,118*

enhanced its focus on maturing plans and processes to better serve survivors and communities; becoming an expeditionary organization that ensures the right people and resources are in the right places at the right times to provide appropriate services to disaster survivors; and catalyzing national disaster risk reduction. The Budget is also focused on enhancing FEMA's organizational foundation through building effective management structures. These structures are inseparable from our mission and are critical to its support– whether through building the mission workforce (with a focus on hiring, managing performance, and career development) or through building secure information technology infrastructure that facilitate our response to catastrophic disasters.

FEMA will build on FY 2015 efforts to enhance current business processes, leverage innovative technologies, and improve the delivery of services and the efficient and effective use of available resources. For example, FEMA is transforming its physical workspace by shrinking its facilities footprint and emphasizing mobility, hoteling and telework for its employees as part of the Agency's Workplace Transformation initiative. FEMA is embracing Secretary Johnson's "Strengthening Departmental Unity of Effort" initiative by actively participating in DHS- and Agency-wide formal engagements, such as

A FEMA Disaster Survivor Assistance Team (DSAT) member talks to a resident affected by the tornado that swept through Bessemer, AL

Planning and Budget Reviews, Internal Collaboration meetings, and Strategic Planning and

Assessment evaluations. These engagements ensure resources are being maximized in order to meet the Agency's mission.

In July 2014, FEMA released the 2014-2018 FEMA Strategic Plan that articulates 16 strategic objectives the Agency will accomplish to provide the best possible support to the American people before, during, and after disasters. The Plan was developed with the input of hundreds of FEMA employees and many external stakeholders who are now working together to execute the Plan's five strategic priorities:

- Be survivor-centric in mission and program delivery;
- Become an expeditionary organization;
- Posture and build capability for catastrophic disasters;
- Enable disaster risk reduction nationally; and
- Strengthen FEMA's organizational foundation.

FEMA's resource decisions will be based on achieving the outcomes in the Strategic Plan, beginning with the FY2016 Budget.

Key Responsibilities:

FEMA manages and coordinates the Federal response to and recovery from major domestic disasters and emergencies of all types, in accordance with the *Robert T. Stafford Disaster Relief and Emergency Assistance Act* (P.L. 93-288), as amended. The Agency coordinates programs to improve the effectiveness of emergency response providers at all levels of government to respond to terrorist attacks, major disasters, and other emergencies.

Service to the Public:

Through the Disaster Relief Fund (DRF), FEMA provides individual and public assistance to help families and communities affected by declared disasters to rebuild and recover. Through its State and local grants program and technical assistance, FEMA helps prepare State and local governments to prevent or respond to threats or incidents of terrorism and other events. FEMA also administers hazard mitigation programs and the National Flood Insurance Program (NFIP) that reduce the risk to life and property from floods and other hazards. FEMA stands ready to provide rapid assistance and resources in emergency situations whenever State and local capabilities are overwhelmed or seriously threatened. At disaster locations, FEMA leads Federal response and recovery efforts by providing emergency management expertise and coordinating critical support resources from across the country.

FY 2014 Accomplishments:

Protection and National Preparedness

FEMA's Protection and National Preparedness (PNP) office is responsible for the coordination of preparedness and protection related activities throughout FEMA, including grants, planning, training, exercises, individual and community preparedness, assessments, lessons learned, and continuity of operations and government. Significant FY 2014 accomplishments include:

- FEMA's Emergency Management Institute (EMI) continued to serve as the emergency management community's flagship training institution for Federal, State, local, tribal, territorial, volunteer, and private sector officials. In 2014, EMI trained more than two million students through in-person or online classes.

First responders train using specialized PPE during a simulated mass casualty incident as a part of a CDP exercise.

- FEMA's Integrated Public Awareness Wireless System (IPAWS) Wireless Emergency Alerts (WEA) aided in the recovery of 13 children as a result of disseminated AMBER Alerts.

- The Center for Domestic Preparedness (CDP) provided specialized, all-hazards preparedness training for domestic emergency responders. To date, the CDP has trained more than 854,000 students.

Office of Response and Recovery

FEMA's Office of Response and Recovery (ORR) coordinates and delivers disaster response and recovery support to citizens and State, local, tribal, and territorial governments. ORR processes all gubernatorial and tribal requests for emergency declarations and major disasters to be declared by the President. Significant FY2014 accomplishments include:

Response

- Supported 48 major disaster declarations, six emergency declarations, and led the activation of the National Response Coordination Center for five major incidents (34 days of operations) and an additional nine incidents (117 days of Enhanced Watch operations) in FY 2014.

- Established an authoritative CORDS (Cadre Operational Readiness and Deployability Status) Report that demonstrates cadre preparedness across staffing, equipping, and training metrics.

- Conducted major Urban Search and Rescue (US&R) response operations that included the Arkansas tornado and the Oso, Washington mudslide.

Recovery

- Obligated over $5.4 billion for Public Assistance including funding to clear debris and rebuild roads, schools, libraries, and other public facilities.

- Provided $84 million in Individual Assistance (IA) services to 160,101 applicants, including housing, crisis counseling, legal services, disaster case management, and unemployment assistance.

Mission Support

Mission Support provides leadership oversight and core operational services for FEMA's day-to-day functionality. Significant FY2014 accomplishments include:

- Conducted the first comprehensive Cyber Security and Resiliency review to ensure FEMA's Resiliency in the Nation's time of need.-

- Achieved $8 million in savings as a result of the FEMA-wide Workplace Transformation initiative; cited as the best example of a GSA-agency partnership for workplace transformation by the National Science Foundation.

- Established the Workforce Management Initiative to develop tools and recommendations to build, manage, and strengthen the Agency's workforce.

Federal Insurance and Mitigation Administration

Federal Insurance and Mitigation Administration (FIMA) strengthens communities' resilience to disasters through risk analysis, risk reduction, and risk insurance. Significant FY2014 accomplishments include:

- Awarded $991 million in Hazard Mitigation Assistance grants to protect life and property in future disasters.

- Recruited, trained, and deployed approximately 480 Hazard Mitigation (HM) Cadre members with an additional 316 anticipated in 2015.

U.S. Fire Administration

The United States Fire Administration (USFA) programs promote fire awareness, safety, and risk reduction across the whole community through training in evaluating and minimizing community risk; improving protection of critical infrastructure; and responding to all-hazard emergencies. Significant FY2014 accomplishments include:

- Received the DHS High Performance and Sustainable Buildings Award in 2014 for implementing innovative strategies and technologies to improve the efficiency of aging infrastructure.

- Trained 84,264 people in fire prevention and control.

BUDGET REQUEST

Dollars in Thousands

	FY 2014 Revised Enacted		FY 2015 Request		FY 2016 Request		FY 2016 +/- FY 2015	
	FTE	$0	FTE	$0	FTE	$0	FTE	$0
Salaries and Expenses	3,829	946,982	4,041	924,664	4,126	949,296	85	24,632
State and Local Programs	212	1,500,000	239	2,225,469	240	2,231,424	1	5,955
Emergency Management Performance Grants[1]	-	350,000	-	-	-	-	-	-
Firefighter Assistance Grants [1]	-	680,000	-	-	-	-	-	-
United States Fire Administration	124	44,000	134	41,407	134	41,582	-	175
Collections – Radiological Emergency Preparedness	153	-13	170	-1,815	170	-305	-	1,510
Disaster Relief Fund	4,893	6,220,908	7,134	7,033,465	7,134	7,374,693	-	341,228
Flood Hazard Mapping and Risk Analysis Program	44	95,202	57	84,403	57	278,625	-	194,222
National Pre-Disaster Mitigation Fund	3	25,000	3	-	10	200,001	7	200,001
Emergency Food and Shelter	-	120,000	-	100,000	-	100,000	-	-
Transfer to OIG	-	-24,000	-	-24,000	-	-24,000	-	-
Transfer to ICE	-	-28,526	-	-	-	-	-	-
Net Discretionary	**9,258**	**9,626,063**	**11,778**	**10,183,593**	**11,871**	**10,801,317**	**93**	**617,724**
National Flood Insurance Fund (Discretionary offsetting collections)	279	173,272	331	179,294	349	181,198	18	1,904
Gross Discretionary	**9,537**	**9,799,335**	**12,109**	**10,362,887**	**12,220**	**$10,982,515**	**111**	**619,628**
National Flood Insurance Fund Mandatory	22	3,174,289	31	3,519,699	32	3,503,574	1	-16,125
National Flood Insurance Reserve Fund	-	122,133	-	522,060	-	980,925	-	458,865
Rescission of Unobligated Balances [2]	-	[-303,490]	-	[-200,000]	-	[-350,000]	-	[-150,000]
Total Budget Authority	**9,559**	**13,095,757**	**12,140**	**$14,404,646**	**12,252**	**$15,467,014**	**112**	**$1,062,368**

[1] Amounts for EMPG and AFG are included in SALP for FY 2015 and FY 2016

[2] Pursuant to P L 113-76, $303 490 million was rescinded in FY 2014: Disaster Relief Fund (Base) - $300 522 million, Office of Domestic Preparedness -$682 8 thousand, National Pre-Disaster Mitigation Fund - $1 577 million, and $708 thousand in lapsed S&E funds The FY 2015 Request included a proposal to cancel $200M in DRF base balances In FY 2016, the Administration proposes to rescind $250 million from DRF base balances and $100 million in unobligated funds from the Community Disaster Loan program

FY 2016 Highlights:

The FY 2016 Budget funds programs that help to ensure that, as a Nation, we are prepared at the Federal, State, and local levels to effectively and rapidly respond to and recover from a variety of disasters.

- **Disaster Relief Fund (DRF)** ....$341M (0 FTE)
  The FY 2016 President's Budget provides $7.37 billion for the DRF, an amount sufficient to cover the FY 2016 estimated requirements for all past declared catastrophic events, including Hurricane Sandy and the 10-year average obligation level for non-catastrophic disaster activity (under $500 million). Through the DRF, FEMA provides a significant portion of the total Federal response to Presidentially-declared major disasters and emergencies.

- **Pre-Disaster Mitigation (PDM)**...$200M (7 FTE)
  The Budget includes $200 million in competitive grants to State, local and tribal governments through the Pre-Disaster Mitigation program. This program provides grants for eligible mitigation planning and projects that reduce disaster losses and protect life and property from future disaster damages. This enhancement supports the President's Climate Action Plan, the FY 2016 Climate Resilience Initiative, and recommendations made by the State, Local, and Tribal Leaders Climate Resilience Task Force.

- **Salaries and Expenses (S&E)**...**$25M (85 FTE)**
  The Budget includes funding for initiatives that enhance FEMA's ability to support citizens and first responders. Additional funding supports efforts to strengthen grants management systems, modernize and increase resiliency of information technology systems, enhance the reliability of the Integrated Public Alert and Warning System (IPAWS), and continue critical capital enhancements for the Mount Weather Emergency Operations Center (MWEOC).

- **Flood Hazard Mapping and Risk Analysis Program**...........................**$194M (0 FTE)**
  The Budget includes an additional $194 million for flood mapping and associated essential tools in educating communities about flood risk and minimizing the loss of life and property at the local level. The flood mapping enhancement also supports the President's Climate Action Plan, the FY 2016 Climate Resilience Initiative, and recommendations made by the State, Local, and Tribal Leaders Climate Resilience Task Force.

U.S. CITIZENSHIP AND IMMIGRATION SERVICES

Description:

United States Citizenship and Immigration Services (USCIS) processes millions of immigration benefit applications every year through a network of approximately 226 domestic and foreign offices.

During FY 2014, USCIS accomplished the following:

- Processed more than 6.7 million applications and petitions;
- Naturalized 655,505 new citizens, of whom 9,526 were military service members along with their qualified family members;
- Managed more than 28 million queries through the E-verify program, up from nearly 25 million in FY 2013;
- Conducted more than 30,000 fraud investigations;
- Interviewed and performed security checks for approximately 67,000 refugee applicants from around the world; and
- Completed nearly 29,000 affirmative asylum applications.

At a Glance	
Senior Leadership:	
León Rodríguez, Director	
Established: 2003	
Major Divisions: Field Operations; Service Center Operations; Refugee, Asylum, and International Operations; Fraud Detection and National Security; Customer Service and Public Engagement; Enterprise Services; and Management.	
Budget Request:	***$4,003,638,000***
Gross Discretionary:	*$ 129,671,000*
Mandatory, Fees	
& Trust Fund:	*$3,873,967,000*
Employees (FTE):	*17,082*

Responsibilities:

Naturalization ceremony held at Mt. Rainier National Park on July 21, 2014.

USCIS ensures that information and decisions on citizenship and immigration benefit requests are provided to customers in a timely, accurate, consistent, courteous, and professional manner, while also working to safeguard our national security. More than 50 different types of citizenship and immigration benefit applications are processed by USCIS. Every case is unique and requires specialized attention from experienced USCIS immigration officers.

Concurrent with its benefits adjudication responsibilities and as an integral part of the examinations process, USCIS employees determine whether individuals or organizations requesting immigration benefits pose a threat to national security, public safety, or the integrity of the Nation's immigration system by:

- Detecting, deterring, and administratively investigating immigration benefit fraud;
- Identifying and eliminating systemic vulnerabilities in the immigration system;
- Implementing effective and efficient security screening policies, programs, and procedures; and
- Promoting information sharing and collaboration with law enforcement and other governmental agencies.

These activities enhance the integrity of our country's legal immigration system, and help combat unauthorized employment and the unauthorized practice of immigration law.

USCIS also fulfills our Nation's humanitarian commitments in accordance with U.S. law and international obligations by extending protection to refugees outside the United States and asylum seekers within the country.

Service to the Public:

USCIS secures America's promise as a Nation of immigrants in many ways by:

- Granting citizenship and immigration benefits,
- Promoting awareness and understanding of citizenship,
- Developing and promoting educational tools and resources for those seeking to become citizens,
- Ensuring the integrity of the immigration system, and
- Providing accurate and useful information to its customers.

Naturalization ceremony held at the Great Hall, Department of Justice, on July 22, 2014. Candidates for citizenship represented 52 countries.

USCIS ensures that immigration benefits are granted only to eligible applicants and petitioners. Its anti-fraud efforts make it easier for employers to comply with labor and immigration law and harder for those seeking to exploit our systems. Additionally, USCIS facilitates the apprehension of criminals across the country through security checks on persons seeking citizenship and immigration benefits.

FY 2014 Accomplishments:

- Processed more than 26,500 Applications to Extend/Change Nonimmigrant Status (Form I-539) and Immigrant Petition by Alien Entrepreneur (Form I-526) applications, and issued more than 454,000 Permanent Resident Cards through the USCIS Electronic Immigration System (ELIS).

- Interviewed and performed security checks for 66,870 refugee applicants in more than 56 countries to support the admission of 69,987 refugees to the United States (who were interviewed in FY 2014 or earlier); completed 28,972 affirmative asylum applications, including 861 filed by unaccompanied children primarily from Central America; and kept pace with incoming credible fear referrals by processing 48,637 credible fear cases.

- Hosted 43 national stakeholder engagements and more than 2,700 local engagements reaching more than 694,000 individuals.

- Continued accepting requests for consideration of Deferred Action for Childhood Arrivals (DACA), thereby supporting DHS immigration enforcement priorities of ensuring that investigation resources are not spent pursuing the removal of low-priority cases involving productive young people. In FY 2014, more than 135,000 individuals were approved for DACA and more than 22,000 were approved for DACA renewal.

- Awarded nearly $10 million in grants to 40 organizations from 24 states and the District of Columbia to support citizenship preparation services for an additional 32,000 permanent residents over a 2-year period.

- Added more than 70,000 additional employers to the E-Verify program, growing to 553,628 employer participants at the end of FY 2014, with an average of more than 1,300 new employers joining each week. The number of employee work authorization verification requests processed grew to more than 28 million in FY 2014.

- Developed myE-Verify, a suite of online services available to U.S. workers who want to check their work authorization status and manage other tasks related to E-Verify. Through myE-Verify, employees can protect against the fraudulent use of their identity by locking their social security numbers, confirm their employment eligibility information, and obtain more detailed information on how to correct their records in the case of a mismatch.

- Processed more than 22.7 million immigration status queries from public benefit-granting agencies (including Federal agencies, State Departments of Motor Vehicles (DMVs), and State and local social service agencies) through the Systematic Alien Verification for Entitlements (SAVE) program to assist these agencies in ensuring that only qualified applicants receive public benefits and licenses. Increased the total customer base by 49 agencies.

- Instituted an intelligence-based methodology for prioritizing national security cases, providing USCIS adjudicators and immigration officers with a more accurate and detailed understanding of potential threats. As a result, USCIS will be able to prioritize and resolve national security cases earlier and more efficiently.

BUDGET REQUEST

Dollars in Thousands

	FY 2014 Revised Enacted		FY 2015 President's Request		FY 2016 President's Request		FY 2016 +/- FY 2015	
	FTE	$000	FTE	$000	FTE	$000	FTE	$000
Salaries and Expenses	388	$116,389	398	$134,755	398	$129,671	---	($5,084)
Gross Discretionary	**388**	**$116,389**	**398**	**$134,755**	**398**	**$129,671**	**---**	**($5,084)**
Immigration Examinations Fee Account	13,228	$3,186,864	14,728	$3,580,771[1]	16,499	$3,813,967[1]	1,771	$233,196
Fraud Prevention and Detection Account	185	$52,552	185	$41,000	185	$45,000	---	$4,000
H-1B Nonimmigrant Petitioner Account	---	$13,000	---	$13,500	---	$15,000	---	$1,500
Subtotal, Mandatory	**13,413**	**$3,252,416**	**14,913**	**$3,635,271**	**16,684**	**3,873,967**	**1,771**	**$238,696**
Less prior-year Rescissions		($1,906)						
Total	**13,801**	**$3,366,899**	**15,311**	**$3,770,026**	**17,082**	**$4,003,638**	**1,771**	**$233,612**

FY 2016 Highlights:

- **E-Verify** .... **$119.7M (398 FTE)**
  E-Verify is an Internet-based program that enables an employer to determine an employee's eligibility to work in the United States by verifying information reported on the employee's Form I-9 against DHS, Social Security Administration, Department of State data, and DMV data from participating States. In FY 2016, USCIS will continue Verification Modernization development to increase the scalability of the Verification Information System—the underlying technology that supports E-Verify—for future expansion. USCIS will also expand access to new data systems, which will enhance E-Verify's ability to quickly and accurately determine an individual's immigration status and employment eligibility. USCIS will continue to leverage partnerships with State DMVs in an effort to execute agreements in support of the RIDE initiative, which helps to prevent identity fraud in E-Verify by verifying the authenticity of drivers' licenses with the issuing state. Finally, USCIS will increase the use of E-Verify fraud and misuse detection tools and continue working on the final non-confirmation appeals process.

- **Transformation and USCIS ELIS (funded from premium processing fee collections)** .... **$199.3M (0 FTE)**
  In FY 2016, the Office of Transformation Coordination (OTC) will deliver a Transformation investment release every 4–6 months utilizing agile development. With each agile release, OTC intends to provide additional capabilities to e-file and adjudicate applications. In FY 2016, OTC will focus on new capabilities addressing Family-based Adjustment of Status, Provisional Waivers, EB-5 Program, and Employment-based Adjustments of Status.

---

[1]Includes funding generated by revenue from the Executive Action on Immigration Reform.

FEDERAL LAW ENFORCEMENT TRAINING CENTER

Description:

Over the past 45 years, the Federal Law Enforcement Training Center (FLETC) has grown into the Nation's largest provider of law enforcement training. Under the consolidated training model, FLETC's Federal partner organizations deliver training unique to their missions, while FLETC provides training in areas common to all law enforcement officers, such as firearms, driving, tactics, investigations, and legal training. Partner agencies realize quantitative and qualitative benefits from this model, including the efficiencies inherent in shared services, higher quality training, and improved interoperability. FLETC's mission is to train all those who protect the homeland, and therefore, its training audience also includes state, local, and tribal departments throughout the U.S. Additionally, FLETC's impact

At a Glance
Senior Leadership: *Connie L. Patrick, Director*
Established: 1970
Major Divisions: Basic training; advanced and specialized training; state, local, tribal, and international training; law enforcement training curriculum development and management; law enforcement training research
Budget Request: $266,694,000
Employees (FTE): 1,090

extends outside our Nation's borders through international training and capacity-building activities. To ensure the training it offers is up-to-date and relevant to emerging needs, FLETC's curriculum development and review process engages experts from across all levels of law enforcement, and FLETC partners extensively with other agencies and stakeholders in training research and the exchange of best practices to ensure it offers the most effective training subject matter, technologies, and methodologies.

Responsibilities:

As the Nation's primary provider of law enforcement training, FLETC is responsible for offering an efficient training model that delivers the highest quality training possible for those who protect the homeland. FLETC accomplishes this by creating and sustaining a collaborative, multi-agency environment that provides both fiscal and qualitative benefits.

Through the consolidated training model, the Federal Government gains the economic advantages of shared services. At a FLETC location, one Federal agency builds and manages a cafeteria, gymnasium, library, training facilities, classrs, computer laboratories, dormitories, and recreational facilities that all federal partners utilize, rather than the Federal Government procuring and maintaining nearly 100 separate sets of facilities for each of the Federal law enforcement agencies. In addition, consolidated training offers economies of scale, because costs to individual agencies decrease as more agencies train at FLETC.

FLETC must ensure that its training enables law enforcement professionals to perform their duties in the safest possible manner, at the highest possible level of proficiency. Consolidated training provides agencies the qualitative benefits of joint training in consistent, standardized, and accredited programs. By training with colleagues from other agencies, new officers and agents build bonds of trust and develop a common sense of purpose that serves them well as they work across organizational boundaries in their careers. Joint training also promotes interoperability, which leads to increased cooperation and intelligence-sharing in the field. Additionally, FLETC's curriculum development and review process brings together stakeholders from throughout the law enforcement community to share and vet ideas about training content and methodology.

Most of the Federal partner organizations that train with FLETC attend one of its multi-agency basic programs, and then provide their recruits with unique agency-specific follow-on programs at their own academies, the majority of which are co-located at one of FLETC's four domestic training sites. These include FLETC's headquarters and residential training site in Glynco, Georgia, and two additional residential training sites in Artesia, New Mexico, and Charleston, South Carolina, all of which feature classrooms, dining and residence halls, and state-of-the-art facilities for basic and advanced law enforcement training. FLETC also operates a non-residential training site in Cheltenham, Maryland, which provides in-service and requalification training for law enforcement officers and agents in the Washington, D.C. area.

In addition to basic training, FLETC leverages the expertise of its training partners to offer an extensive array of specialized and advanced training programs, including distance learning opportunities. Additionally, through a Memorandum of Understanding with the Port of Los Angeles, FLETC has personnel assigned to deliver training at the Los Angeles Regional Maritime Law Enforcement Training Center in topics focused on protecting America's waterways and ports.

State, local, and tribal law enforcement officers and agents are an integral part of the homeland security community. To reach them, FLETC provides specialized and advanced training at its domestic training sites, and provides on-site training programs to State, local and tribal agencies throughout the country. Finally, FLETC serves DHS's international mission through participation and leadership in the International Law Enforcement Academies, training and capacity-building activities overseas, hosting international law enforcement personnel at FLETC's domestic training sites, and engaging with international partners in research and the exchange of best practices and subject matter expertise.

Service to the Public:

FLETC's mission is to train those who protect the homeland. FLETC's federally accredited law enforcement training programs constitute a source of career-long training for the worldwide law enforcement community, which enables officers and agents to fulfill their responsibilities safely and proficiently. FLETC's contributions to law enforcement training research, management, and curriculum development help foster the continued professionalism of law enforcement. Well-prepared law enforcement officers and agents are able to operate more safely and effectively. This ultimately leads to a safer and more secure American public.

Law enforcement officers participate in training at FLETC's Forensic Science Training Complex.

Law Enforcement officers participate in marksmanship training using FLETC's Virtual Range.

FY 2014 Accomplishments:

- Effectively trained 58,666 law enforcement personnel, including 5,897 state and local law enforcement officers and 851 international law enforcement personnel.

- Achieved re-accreditation status for the Firearms Instructor Training Program, and maintained accreditation status and program accreditation for 12 training programs.

- Hosted three Curriculum Development Conferences to develop new programs to meet emergent needs, including the Leadership in a Crisis Training Program, Department of State Foreign Affairs Counter Threat Training Program, and Smart Phone Analysis Training Program.

- In response to a DHS mandate to develop standardized tactical medical care training, piloted the Basic Tactical Medical Training Program.

- Partnered with the Inspector General (IG) Criminal Investigator Academy in the design, testing, and deployment of tablets in its advanced training programs.

- Through collaboration with the U.S. Courts, completed the Glynco Courtroom Modernization project, providing state-of-the-art courtroom technology.

- In support of the President's Plan to Reduce Gun Violence, expanded active threat training by more than 700 percent, training 2,428 law enforcement officers throughout the U.S.

- Developed a comprehensive strategic plan to develop and implement FLETC's Online Campus, a virtual learning environment that will help the Department realize efficiencies by avoiding duplication of existing online training infrastructure and will increase interoperability of law enforcement through shared training and information-sharing.

- Conducted 90 webcasts, reaching more than 8,000 participants in various legal topics.

- Partnered with the Department of Justice and academia to bring together subject-matter experts from a variety of disciplines to participate in summits aimed at developing strategic approaches to preventing multiple casualty violence and countering violent extremism.

- Worked with U.S. Immigration and Customs Enforcement to establish temporary housing facilities at FLETC's training site in Artesia, New Mexico, for females and minor children apprehended after unlawfully crossing the Southern Border.

- Delivered seven iterations of the Women in Law Enforcement Leadership Program domestically and internationally to 204 female law enforcement leaders from 24 countries.

- Established a FLETC training presence at the Los Angeles Regional Maritime Law Enforcement Training Center in support of protecting U.S. waterways and ports.

- Effectively trained approximately 1,800 students in basic marksmanship using the Virtual Range Complex, avoiding the firing of approximately 488,400 live rounds of ammunition and the related costs of cleanup and range repair.

- Supported countering human trafficking training in seven countries and produced nine new training videos and two new online training programs in support of the DHS Blue Campaign.

- Through a Memorandum of Agreement with the National Protection and Programs Directorate, Federal Protective Service, established a "Protection Center of Excellence," which will serve the protection communities of interest by identifying, developing, and delivering training courses based on the standards and guidelines established by the Interagency Security Committee.

- To fully support implementation of Presidential Policy Directive 23, Security Sector Assistance, established a liaison position at the Department of Justice to coordinate harmonization among the departments and ensure effective delivery of law enforcement training within DHS and the interagency.

BUDGET REQUEST
Dollars in Thousands

	FY 2014 Revised Enacted		FY 2015 President's Budget		FY 2016 President's Budget[2]		FY 2016 +/- FY 2015	
	FTE	$000	FTE	$000	FTE	$000	FTE	$000
Salaries and Expenses, FLETC	1,051	$226,545	1,068	$230,454	1,083	$237,830	(2)	$7,376
Salaries and Expenses, FLETA	7	$1,300	7	$1,300	7	$1,311	-	$11
Acquisition, Construction, Improvements & Related Expenses	-	$30,885		$27,841		$27,553	-	$(288)
Net Discretionary	**1,058**	**$258,730**	**1,075**	**$259,595**	**1,090**	**$266,694**	**(2)**	**$7,099**
Total Budget Authority	**1,058**	**$258,730**	**1,075**	**$259,595**	**1,090**	**$266,694**	**(2)**	**$7,099**
Less prior year Rescissions [1]		$(390)				-		-
Total		**$258,340**		**$258,556**		**$266,694**		**$7,099**

1 Rescission of prior year balances pursuant to P.L 113-76

2 Includes a transfer of $7,000 to Office of Chief Information Officer for data center costs.

FY 2016 Highlights:

- **Train Additional CBP Officers** .... **$26.4M (39 FTE)**
  FLETC will provide basic training for up to 2,000 new U.S. Customs and Border Protection (CBP) Officers proposed in the President's 2015 Budget in continued support of the President's initiatives on promoting travel and trade.

SCIENCE AND TECHNOLOGY DIRECTORATE

Description:

The Science and Technology (S&T) Directorate's mission is to improve homeland security by working with partners to provide state-of-the-art technology and solutions that help them to achieve their missions. S&T partners and customers include the operating Components of the Department, as well as State, local, tribal, and territorial emergency responders and officials.

Responsibilities:

S&T accomplishes its mission through partner-focused and outcome-oriented Research, Development, Acquisitions, and Operations (RDA&O) programs that balance risk, cost, impact, and time to delivery. These RDA&O programs support the needs of the operational Components of the Department and the first responder community. S&T develops state-of-the-art solutions to protect the Nation's people and critical infrastructure from chemical, biological, explosive, and cyber attacks, as well as provides new solutions to protect the borders and address crosscutting areas such as standards and interoperability. Through Management and Administration (M&A), S&T funds the effective and efficient management and leadership of Directorate activities to deliver advanced technology solutions to DHS Components and first responders.

S&T ensures that DHS and the homeland security community have the science, technical information, and capabilities they need to effectively and efficiently prevent, protect against, respond to, and recover from all-hazards and homeland security threats.

At a Glance
Senior Leadership: *Under Secretary Reginald Brothers, PhD*
Established: 2003
Major Divisions: First Responders Group, Homeland Security Advanced Research Projects Agency, Capabilities Development Support, and Research & Development Partnerships
Budget Request: $778,988,000
Employees (FTE): 472

Left: Commercial Aircraft Vulnerability and Mitigation Project
Provides a blast mitigation option for wide body aircraft operators at a weight that is within the range of comparable size non-blast resistant containers currently in use.

Middle: Wide Area Surveillance Project
The Imaging System for Immersive Surveillance 360° field of view camera head, including an example of the 360° full field of view.

Right: Canine Explosives Detection Project
Training aids for the Explosive Detection Dog (EDD) that can be employed throughout the entire Homeland Security Enterprise community, including federal, state and local partners.

The Directorate has four RDA&O Programs, Projects, and Activities (PPA), each of which has an important role in implementing research, development, testing, and evaluation (RDT&E) activities. These PPAs are Research, Development, & Innovation; Acquisition and Operations Support; Laboratory Facilities; and University Programs.

Research, Development, and Innovation (RD&I)

RD&I provides state-of-the-art technology and solutions to meet the needs of the operational Components of the Department and the first responder community. RD&I includes customer-focused and outcome-oriented RDT&E programs that balance risk, cost, impact, and time to delivery.

Acquisition and Operations Support (AOS)

AOS provides expert assistance to entities across the Homeland Security Enterprise (HSE) to ensure that the transition, acquisition, and deployment of technologies, information, and procedures improve the efficiency and effectiveness of the operational capabilities across the HSE mission.

Laboratory Facilities

The Office of National Laboratories (ONL) manages the Laboratory Facilities programs. ONL provides the Nation with coordinated, productive science, technology, and engineering laboratories, organizations, and institutions, which can provide the knowledge and technology required to secure the homeland.

University Programs

University Programs supports critical homeland security-related research and education at U.S. colleges and universities to address high-priority, DHS-related issues and to enhance homeland security capabilities over the long term.

Service to the Public:

S&T is central to securing the homeland and providing leadership to harness science and technology while encouraging public and private-sector innovation – in coordination and partnership with universities, research institutes and laboratories, other government agencies, and private-sector companies – to counter threats and hazards. Science and technology improvements have helped to ensure the Nation's safety, and continue to be deployed to protect the homeland.

FY 2014 Accomplishments:

- **Canine Explosives Detection** – Developed non-hazardous, low-cost homemade explosive (HME) training aids for the Explosive Detection Dog (EDD) program that can be employed throughout the entire homeland security community, including Federal, State and local partners. These training aids represent a paradigm shift in the way that communities can establish and maintain operational proficiency in a cost effective manner.

- **BioAssays** – Transitioned a suspension bead assay for laboratory-based detection of Abrin, a substance significantly more toxic than Ricin. Abrin is easily made from the seeds of a plant that grows wild in warm temperature and tropical regions of the world, and is found in the southern areas of the United States. This assay closed a gap that existed with respect to the detection of this toxin within the biodefense community.

- **Risk-based Resource Deployment Decision-aid (R2D2)** – Transitioned R2D2 to the Federal Air Marshal Service. R2D2 applies a risk calculation to the deployment of Air Marshal resources to air, land, and water security assignments. Intensive work with end users resulted in a product that includes geospatial visualization, temporal filtering, flight route characteristic filtering, and airport (departure and arrival) filtering that allows analysis of various forms of protective resource deployment.

- **Next-Generation Incident Command System (NICS)** – Completed the development of NICS, a common platform to share standards-based data with real-time collaboration and on-line white-boarding across the first responder community. NICS has been extensively used by California Department of Forestry and Fire Protection (CAL FIRE) for wildland fire management to collaborate, pool resources, and plot strategies for their response to wildland fires. A total of 2,500+ users and over 500 organizations comprise the NICS community. Internationally, NICS was adopted by the Australia's Emergency Management Community (State of Victoria).

- **Commercial Aircraft Vulnerability and Mitigation** – Developed an improved blast-resistant container that can be used for the transport of checked passenger luggage and air cargo contents onboard wide body commercial aircraft. The Hardened Unit Load Device (HULD-R) provides a blast mitigation option for wide body aircraft operators at a weight that is within the range of comparable size non-blast resistant containers currently in use.

- **Rapid DNA** – Delivered two Rapid DNA systems to Customs and Border Protection (CBP). This new capability provides CBP with a cost-effective and highly accurate measure of establishing family relationships in an environment that is extremely time sensitive. CBP can now identify family members in question with 99.4-percent accuracy within 90 minutes.

- **Wide Area Surveillance Program** – Demonstrated the Imaging System for Immersive Surveillance. This system uses multiple cameras that provide continuous, high resolution 360° coverage of a scene. Using advanced video processing algorithms, information from multiple cameras is fused to create a single stitched image. In 2014, the system was successfully demonstrated and utilized by the Boston Police Department at the 2014 Boston Marathon, providing coverage to the finish line and at Kenmore Square.

Budget Request
Dollars in Thousands

	FY 2014 Revised Enacted		FY 2015 President's Budget		FY 2016 President's Budget		FY 2016 +/- FY 2015	
	FTE	$000	FTE	$000	FTE	$000	FTE	$000
Management and Administration	334	129,000	337	130,147	342	132,115	5	1,968
Acquisition and Operations Support	-	41,703		41,703		47,102	-	5,399
Laboratory Facilities	123	547,785	130	435,180	130	133,921	-	(301,259)
Research, Development, and Innovation	-	462,000		433,788		434,850	-	1,062
University Programs	-	39,724		31,000		31,000	-	-
Gross Discretionary	457	1,220,212	467	1,071,818	472	778,988	5	(292,830)
Total Budget Authority	457	1,220,212	467	1,071,818	472	778,988	5	(292,830)
Less prior year Rescissions	-	(133)	-	-	-	-	-	-
Total	457	1,220,079	467	1,071,818	472	778,988	5	(292,830)

FY 2016 Highlights:

- **Apex Program**..$45.2M (0 FTE)
  The Apex program has been very successful and has generated a full range of lessons learned including front-end assessment and capability base-lining, working jointly with DHS operational partners, and joint program execution. The new expanded Apex projects will be cross-cutting, multi-disciplinary efforts intended to solve problems of strategic operational importance. The projects are being scaled to apply to a wider portion of S&T's research

portfolio and will operate on five-year timelines. The new Apexes will include some current efforts rolled up with expanded or new ones. With high-profile projects, concrete deliverables, precise milestones and timelines, and significant increases in dollar and workforce investment, the new, scaled Apex efforts will bring substantial gains for S&T's operational partners involved with cargo and passenger screening, border security, network security, flood resilience, biodetection, and emergency response.

- **Apex Engines**...**$18.0M (0 FTE)**
  This project provides support through cross-cutting, multi-use technologies and functions that will provide the same services to all Apex programs and to S&T at large, but tailored based on the Apex program's individual focus and capability needs. The Engines will provide best practices, reusable products and solutions, lessons learned, and technical services to respond rapidly and provide technical subject matter expertise to the Apex programs and other projects and cross-cutting initiatives. The Engines enable S&T to apply its skills and promote common approaches and solutions that are tailored to S&T programs, component sponsors across program areas and throughout the HSE. The Engines accomplish this by collaborating with external scientific, technical, industrial and academic communities, proactively monitoring trends for emerging capabilities and maintaining an in-depth understanding of state-of-the-art techniques in specific capability areas.

- **Biosurveillance Systems**...**$7.1M (0 FTE)**
  This project enhances and tests existing affordable and effective environmental sensors to identify incremental improvements to sensor technologies for use in urban areas for biological event detection and characterization. The information from these sensors and other data sources will be assembled with data fusion concepts to build CONOPS with strong coordination in the Federal interagency and local communities.

- **Integrated Passenger Screening Systems**...**$19.3M (0 FTE)**
  This project reduces inconvenience to passengers with the increased capability to respond to evolving threats at current or reduced system costs. Modular, flat panel Advanced Imaging Technology AIT solutions will provide a less expensive, more flexible solution for passenger screening and potentially reduces the need for passengers to remove articles of clothing during screening.

- **Bio-Threat Characterization**..**$ 7.0M (0 FTE)**
  This project provides knowledge products (technical reports) generated through laboratory experiments to understand the critical physical, chemical, and physiological parameters associated with potential bioterrorism agents and emerging infectious diseases. The project also develops tools to link genetic information of potential threat agents to characteristics associated with a pathogen's risk to human or agricultural assets thereby improving pre-event planning and event specific operational decisions.

- **Plum Island Animal Disease Center Operations**................................**$2.4M (0 FTE)**
  This project allows Plum Island Animal Disease Center Operations (PIADC) to remain in compliance with the bio-containment waste management requirements of the New York State Department of Environmental Conservation (DEC). Funding also support's PIADC's efforts to meet the U.S. Department of Agriculture's new select agent Tier one requirements for high threat biologic select agents, such as foot and mouth disease. These new

requirements mandate strengthened security monitoring (cameras), intrusion detection and screening (x-ray and metal detectors), and occupation health medical evaluations of staff. Additional funds will also be used to focus on waste characterization and management requirements in order to minimize the potential for enforcement actions (e.g. fines, suspension of permits) as a result of noncompliance.

FY 2016 Major Decreases:

- **National Bio and Agro-Defense Facility Program Construction........-$300.0M (0 FTE)**
  This decrease is the result of the Department receiving full funding for the National Bio and Agro-Defense Facility (NBAF) construction in FY 2015.

DOMESTIC NUCLEAR DETECTION OFFICE

Description:

The Domestic Nuclear Detection Office (DNDO) leads the development of the Global Nuclear Detection Architecture (GNDA), implements its domestic component, and leads the integration of United States Government (USG) technical nuclear forensics capabilities.

Responsibilities:

DNDO is the lead agency within the USG charged with development of the GNDA and the implementation of its domestic component, as well as coordination and stewardship of USG technical nuclear forensics efforts. DNDO works closely with Federal, State, local, tribal, international, and partners in academia and the private sector. Functions include integrating interagency efforts to develop and acquire radiological and nuclear (rad/nuc) detection technologies, evaluating detector performance, ensuring effective response to detection alarms, integrating and ensuring readiness of U.S. nuclear forensics capabilities, and conducting transformational research and development for rad/nuc detection and forensics technologies. For both the detection and forensics missions, the likelihood of success is maximized by placing the appropriate technologies in the hands of well-trained law enforcement, public safety officials and scientists, for application in operations that are driven by intelligence indicators.

> ### At a Glance
>
> Senior Leadership:
> Dr. Huban A. Gowadia, Director
> Dr. L. Wayne Brasure, Deputy Director
>
> Established: 2005
>
> Major Divisions: Architecture and Plans Directorate, Transformational and Applied Research Directorate, Product Acquisition and Deployment Directorate, Systems Engineering and Evaluation Directorate, Operations Support Directorate, National Technical Nuclear Forensics Center, Red Team and Net Assessments
>
> **Budget Request: $357, 327,000**
>
> Employees (FTE): 137

Service to the Public:

DNDO works to protect the United States from rad/nuc terrorism by developing, acquiring, and deploying detection technologies, supporting operational law enforcement and homeland security partners, and by continuing to integrate technical nuclear forensic programs and advancing the state-of-the-art in nuclear forensics technologies. In order to address gaps in the implemented GNDA and dramatically improve the performance of rad/nuc detection and technical nuclear forensic technologies, DNDO also invests in basic, applied, and developmental research to identify, explore, develop, and demonstrate new and innovative technologies. As part of the effort to foster and maintain expertise in specialized technical fields related to nuclear detection and forensics, DNDO supports academic programs, scholarships, and fellowships to advance research and encourage students in these fields of study. In addition, DNDO seeks to improve effectiveness of deployed technology through improved operational concepts. DNDO works with Federal, State, local, and tribal partners, to ensure that rad/nuc detection capabilities provide the greatest level of protection possible through multiple layers of defense.

FY 2014 Accomplishments:

- Procured radiation detection equipment for operators, in accordance with joint acquisition strategies planned with U.S. Customs and Border Protection (CBP), U.S. Coast Guard (USCG), and the Transportation Security Administration (TSA).

- Initiated the Securing the Cities efforts in the National Capital Region, which is the third implementation of the program.

- Led the interagency in successfully delivering the 2014 Joint Annual Interagency Review of the GNDA, involving over 70 programs and projects, and the delivery of the Joint Interagency Annual Review of the National Strategic Five-Year Plan, which also informed the development of the updated *National Strategic Five-Year Plan for Improving the Nuclear Forensics and Attribution Capabilities of the United States*.

- Completed operational testing with USCG and CBP to implement a novel solution for Small Vessel Standoff detection capability. The solution leverages fielded technology, saving development and acquisition costs for new detectors.

- Completed 48 comprehensive evaluations and demonstrations of new and improved technologies to detect nuclear and other radioactive materials.

- Completed over 160 exercises, assessments, and deployments to enhance Federal, State, local, and tribal agencies' readiness to combat nuclear terrorism, reflecting an approximate 60 percent increase over FY 2013 activities.

- Conducted over 20 overt and covert adversary-based assessments of detection operations with Federal, State and local stakeholders.

A law enforcement officer uses radiation detection equipment in a maritime environment in Tampa Bay, Florida as part of the Operation Radiological Operations Preparedness Exercise (ROPE).

- Completed the technology transfer of strontium iodide scintillator material to industry and conducted two feasibility evaluations demonstrating advanced concepts for light readout from scintillation crystals using the latest solid-state technology. Led the Nuclear Forensics Executive Council in clarifying the Foreign Nuclear Forensics Post Nuclear Detonation Collections Requirements. This enabled the U.S. Ground Collections Task Force to create a response plan to support requested assistance resulting from a foreign nuclear detonation.

- Awarded 72 undergraduate, graduate, and post-doctorate fellowships and internships, university and junior faculty awards, and academic research awards in nuclear forensics and radiation detection-related specialties. DNDO is on track to meet the initial milestone of adding 35 new Ph.D. scientists to the nuclear forensics field by 2018.

BUDGET REQUEST
Dollars in Thousands

	FY 2014 Revised Enacted		FY 2015 President's Budget		FY 2016 President's Budget		FY 2016 +/- FY 2015	
	FTE	$000	FTE	$000	FTE	$000	FTE	$000
Management and Administration	121	$38,491	127	$37,494	137	$38,316	10	$822
Research, Development, and Operations	-	$204,164	-	$199,068	-	$196,000	-	($3,068)
Systems Acquisition	-	$45,400	-	$67,861	-	$123,011	-	$55,150
Net Discretionary	**121**	**$288,055**	**127**	**$304,423**	**137**	**$357,327**	**10**	**$52,904**
Gross Discretionary	**121**	**$288,055**	**127**	**$304,423**	**137**	**$357,327**	**10**	**$52,904**
Total Budget Authority	**121**	**$288,055**	**127**	**$304,423**	**137**	**$357,327**	**10**	**$52,904**
Less prior year Rescissions	-	(57)	-	-	-	-	-	-
Total	**121**	**$287,998**	**127**	**$304,423**	**137**	**$357,327**	**10**	**$52,904**

FY 2016 Highlights:

- **Radiological and Nuclear Detection Equipment (RDE) Acquisition....... $44.7M (0 FTE)**
The increased level of funding for Radiological and Nuclear Detection Equipment (RDE) acquisition will support continued Radiation Portal Monitor (RPM) deployment activities at ports of entry while also proactively addressing sustainability concerns with aging fielded systems, including Human Portable Radiation Detection Systems units.

- **Securing the Cities.. $10.0M (0 FTE)**
The Securing the Cities program seeks to assist State, local, and tribal stakeholders to design and implement or enhance existing architectures for coordinated and integrated detection and interdiction of nuclear and radiological materials out of regulatory control within high-risk metropolitan areas. In FY 2016, DNDO's funding request will support ongoing implementation activities for Securing the Cities in three implementation sites (second, third, and fourth regions) and selection of a fifth site based on a full and open competition of eligible cities.

A Transportation Security Administration (TSA) Visible Intermodal Prevention and Response (VIPR) team member carries radiological/nuclear detection equipment in his backpack at Penn Station on January 30, 2014 in New York City. TSA teams augmented local law enforcement to increase visibility at the station, which was a major transportation hub for Super

Resource Tables

Department of Homeland Security
Total Budget Authority

	FY 2015 President's Budget			FY 2016 Total Adjustment to Base			FY 2016 Total Program Changes			FY 2016 President's Budget		
	Pos.	FTE	$$$	Pos.	FTE	$$$	Pos.	FTE	$$$	Pos.	FTE	$$$
Departmental Management and Operations	1,946	1,939	748,024	27	34	(86,966)	81	56	299,569	2,054	2,029	960,627
Office of the Secretary and Executive Management	586	583	128,769	7	10	346	4	4	5,132	597	597	134,247
Office of the Under Secretary for Management (USM):	854	854	195,286	(39)	(39)	(9,146)	14	7	7,047	829	822	193,187
DHS Headquarters Consolidation Project	-	-	73,000	-	-	(61,455)	-	-	204,277	-	-	215,822
Office of the Chief Financial Officer	216	212	94,626	10	14	(41,272)	4	2	43,421	230	228	96,775
Office of the Chief Information Officer (CIO) and Department-wide IT:	290	290	256,343	49	49	24,561	59	43	39,692	398	382	320,596
Net Discretionary	_1,946_	_1,939_	_748,024_	_27_	_34_	_(86,966)_	_81_	_56_	_299,569_	_2,054_	_2,029_	_960,627_
Analysis and Operations	879	850	302,268	(3)	(29)	(50,187)	24	13	17,009	900	834	269,090
Net Discretionary	_879_	_850_	_302,268_	_(3)_	_(29)_	_(50,187)_	_24_	_13_	_17,009_	_900_	_834_	_269,090_
Office of Inspector General	725	725	145,457	-	-	(246)	142	71	21,073	867	796	166,284
Net Discretionary	_725_	_725_	_145,457_	-	-	_(246)_	_142_	_71_	_21,073_	_867_	_796_	_166,284_
U.S. Customs and Border Protection	62,912	61,707	12,764,835	(104)	627	357,191	210	118	443,268	63,018	62,452	13,565,294
Salaries and Expenses	48,209	47,136	8,326,386	(93)	635	565,266	195	103	178,027	48,311	47,874	9,069,679
Automation Modernization:	1,677	1,578	812,410	39	42	26,520	-	-	28,381	1,716	1,620	867,311
Border Security Fencing, Infrastructure, and Technology:	-	-	362,466	-	-	(60,407)	-	-	71,402	-	-	373,461
Air and Marine Interdiction:	1,722	1,719	708,685	-	-	(47,501)	15	15	86,238	1,737	1,734	747,422
Facilities Management	516	486	482,205	(100)	(100)	(219,882)	-	-	79,220	416	386	341,543
Fee accounts:	9,504	9,504	1,886,691	50	50	93,195	-	-	-	9,554	9,554	1,979,886
Trust Fund Accounts:	-	-	5,992	-	-	-	-	-	-	-	-	5,992
COBRA-CFTA	1,284	1,284	180,000	-	-	-	-	-	-	1,284	1,284	180,000
IUF - DISCRETIONARY												
Net Discretionary	_53,477_	_52,272_	_10,880,941_	_(154)_	_577_	_264,304_	_210_	_118_	_443,268_	_53,533_	_52,967_	_11,588,513_
Discretionary Fee Funded	_96_	_96_	_91,192_	-	-	_597_	-	-	-	_96_	_96_	_91,789_
Gross Discretionary	_53,573_	_52,368_	_10,972,133_	_(154)_	_577_	_264,901_	_210_	_118_	_443,268_	_53,629_	_53,063_	_11,680,302_
Mandatory, Fees, Trust Funds	_9,339_	_9,339_	_1,792,702_	_50_	_50_	_92,290_	-	-	-	_9,389_	_9,389_	_1,884,992_
U.S. Immigration and Customs Enforcement	20,972	19,374	5,359,065	3	57	183,405	311	360	739,167	21,286	19,791	6,281,637
Salaries and Expenses	20,585	19,019	4,988,065	3	57	232,405	311	360	660,667	20,899	19,436	5,881,137
Automation Modernization	-	-	26,000	-	-	(26,000)	-	-	73,500	-	-	73,500
Construction	-	-	-	-	-	-	-	-	5,000	-	-	5,000
Fee Accounts:	387	355	345,000	-	-	(23,000)	-	-	-	355	355	322,000
Net Discretionary	_20,585_	_19,019_	_5,014,065_	_3_	_57_	_206,405_	_311_	_360_	_739,167_	_20,899_	_19,436_	_5,959,637_
Mandatory, Fees, Trust Funds	_387_	_355_	_345,000_	_3_	_57_	_(23,000)_	-	-	-	_387_	_355_	_322,000_

Resource Tables

Department of Homeland Security
Total Budget Authority

	FY 2015 President's Budget			FY 2016 Total Adjustment to Base			FY 2016 Total Program Changes			FY 2016 President's Budget		
	Pos.	FTE	$$$	Pos.	FTE	$$$	Pos.	FTE	$$$	Pos.	FTE	$$$
Transportation Security Administration	57,178	52,555	7,305,098	(1)	(5)	156,864	(1,745)	(1,740)	(115,038)	55,432	50,810	7,346,924
Aviation Security:	53,593	49,203	5,683,304	(131)	(131)	41,013	(1,708)	(1,705)	(109,551)	51,754	47,367	5,614,766
Surface Transportation Security:	905	860	127,637	(7)	(7)	467	(37)	(35)	(4,276)	861	818	123,828
Intelligence and Vetting	794	742	312,131	58	57	118,270			(3,550)	852	799	426,851
Transportation Security Support:	1,886	1,750	932,026	79	76	(2,886)			2,339	1,965	1,826	931,479
Federal Air Marshals:												
Net Discretionary	57,096	52,475	4,157,200	(50)	(53)	723,658	(1,745)	(1,740)	(115,038)	55,301	50,682	4,765,820
Discretionary Fee Funded	76	74	2,892,898	40	39	(566,994)				116	113	2,325,904
Gross Discretionary	57,172	52,549	7,050,098	(10)	(14)	156,664	(1,745)	(1,740)	(115,038)	55,417	50,795	7,091,724
Mandatory, Fees, Trust Funds	6	6	255,000	9	9	200				15	15	255,200
U.S. Coast Guard	49,093	49,547	9,810,468	346	(304)	220,370			(66,924)	49,439	49,243	9,963,914
Operating Expenses	47,644	48,116	6,750,733	346	(304)	70,770				47,990	47,812	6,821,503
Environmental Compliance and Restoration	25	24	13,214			55				25	24	13,269
Reserve Training	416	416	109,605			1,009				416	416	110,614
Acquisition, Construction and Improvements	898	881	1,084,193						(66,924)	898	881	1,017,269
Research, Development, Test and Evaluation	96	96	17,947			188				96	96	18,135
Medicare-Eligible Retiree Health Care Fund Contribution			176,970			(17,664)						159,306
Retired Pay			1,443,896			161,526						1,605,422
Boat Safety	14	14	112,830			2,946				14	14	115,776
Maritime Oil Spill Program			101,000									101,000
General Gift Funds			80			1,541						1,621
Net Discretionary	49,079	49,533	8,152,662	346	(304)	54,357			(66,924)	49,425	49,229	8,140,095
Mandatory, Fees, Trust Funds	14	14	1,657,806			166,013				14	14	1,823,819
U.S. Secret Service	6,667	6,572	1,895,905	(30)	46	72,329	57	29	235,888	6,694	6,647	2,204,122
Operating Expenses	6,667	6,572	1,585,970	(30)	46	66,545	57	29	214,938	6,694	6,647	1,867,453
Acquisition, Construction, and Improvements			49,935			784			20,950			71,669
Retired pay (mandatory - trust fund):			260,000			5,000						265,000
Net Discretionary	6,667	6,572	1,635,905	(30)	46	67,329	57	29	235,888	6,694	6,647	1,939,122
Mandatory, Fees, Trust Funds			260,000			5,000						265,000

Department of Homeland Security
Total Budget Authority

	FY 2015 President's Budget			FY 2016 Total Adjustment to Base			FY 2016 Total Program Changes			FY 2016 President's Budget		
	Pos.	FTE	$$$	Pos.	FTE	$$$	Pos.	FTE	$$$	Pos.	FTE	$$$
National Protection & Programs Directorate	3,621	3,463	2,857,666	62	15	(131,024)	94	49	376,220	3,777	3,527	3,102,862
Management and Administration	394	358	65,910	(8)	9	(1,719)				386	367	64,191
Federal Protective Service	1,466	1,371	1,342,606	15	15	100,843				1,481	1,386	1,443,449
Infrastructure Protection and Information Security	1,571	1,544	1,197,566	68	13	(196,297)	94	49	310,420	1,733	1,606	1,311,689
Office of Biometric Identity Management	190	190	251,584	(13)	(22)	(33,851)				177	168	283,533
Net Discretionary	2,155	2,092	1,515,060	47		(231,867)	94	49	376,220	2,296	2,141	1,659,413
Discretionary Fee Funded	1,466	1,371	1,342,606	15	15	100,843				1,481	1,386	1,443,449
Gross Discretionary	3,621	3,463	2,857,666	62	15	(131,024)	94	49	376,220	3,777	3,527	3,102,862
Office of Health Affairs	106	99	125,767	(3)	(3)	(1,698)				103	96	124,069
Net Discretionary	106	99	125,767	(3)	(3)	(1,698)				103	96	124,069
Federal Emergency Management Agency	5,072	12,140	14,404,646	86	95	644,149	23	17	418,218	5,181	12,252	15,467,013
Salaries and Expenses	4,041	4,041	924,664	85	85	10,332			14,300	4,126	4,126	949,296
Emergency Management Performance Grants												
State and Local Programs	239	239	2,225,469	1	1	(45)			6,000	240	240	2,231,424
National Pre-Disaster Mitigation Fund	3	3					13	7	200,001	16	10	200,001
Firefighter Assistance Grants												
United States Fire Administration	134	134	41,407			175				134	134	41,582
Radiological Emergency Preparedness:	170	170	(1,815)			1,510				170	170	(305)
Disaster Relief Fund	55	7,134	6,809,465			289,328			1,900	55	7,134	7,100,693
Disaster Assistance Direct Loan Program						(100,000)						(100,000)
Flood Hazard Mapping and Risk Analysis	57	57	84,403			75			194,147	57	57	278,625
National Flood Insurance Fund	373	362	4,221,053		9	442,774	10	10	1,870	383	381	4,665,697
Emergency Food and Shelter			100,000									100,000
Net Discretionary	4,699	11,778	10,183,593	86	86	201,375	13	7	416,348	4,798	11,871	10,801,316
Discretionary Fee Funded	341	331	179,294	8		34	10	10	1,870	351	349	181,198
Gross Discretionary	5,040	12,109	10,362,887	94	86	201,409	23	17	418,218	5,149	12,220	10,982,514
Mandatory, Fees, Trust Funds	32	31	4,041,759			442,740				32	32	4,484,499
Citizenship & Immigration Services:	17,311	15,311	3,770,026	1,256	1,771	233,612				18,567	17,082	4,003,638
Salaries and Expenses	419	398	134,755			(5,084)				419	398	129,671
Immigration Examinations Fee Account:	16,707	14,728	3,580,771	1,256	1,771	233,196				17,963	16,499	3,813,967
H-1B Nonimmigrant Petitioner Account			13,500			1,500						15,000
Fraud Prevention and Detection Account	185	185	41,000			4,000				185	185	45,000
Net Discretionary	419	398	134,755			(5,084)				419	398	129,671
Mandatory, Fees, Trust Funds	16,892	14,913	3,635,271	1,256	1,771	238,696				18,148	16,684	3,873,967

Department of Homeland Security
Total Budget Authority

	FY 2015 President's Budget			FY 2016 Total Adjustment to Base			FY 2016 Total Program Changes			FY 2016 President's Budget		
	Pos.	FTE	$$$	Pos.	FTE	$$$	Pos.	FTE	$$$	Pos.	FTE	$$$
Federal Law Enforcement Training Center	**1,102**	**1,075**	**259,595**	**(24)**	**(24)**	**(19,307)**	**39**	**39**	**26,406**	**1,117**	**1,090**	**266,694**
Salaries and Expenses	1,102	1,075	231,754	(24)	(24)	(19,019)	39	39	26,406	1,117	1,090	239,141
Acquisition, Construction, Improvements & Related Expenses:			27,841			(288)						27,553
Net Discretionary	1,102	1,075	259,595	(24)	(24)	(19,307)	39	39	26,406	1,117	1,090	266,694
Science & Technology	**467**	**467**	**1,071,818**	**(1)**	**(1)**	**(300,218)**	**6**	**6**	**7,388**	**472**	**472**	**778,988**
Management and Administration:	337	337	130,147	(1)	(1)	(533)	6	6	2,501	342	342	132,115
Research, Development, Acquisitions, and Operations	**130**	**130**	**941,671**	-	-	**(299,685)**	-	-	**4,887**	**130**	**130**	**646,873**
Net Discretionary	467	467	1,071,818	(1)	(1)	(300,218)	6	6	7,388	472	472	778,988
Domestic Nuclear Detection Office	**127**	**127**	**304,423**	**10**	**10**	**305**	-	-	**52,599**	**137**	**137**	**357,327**
Management and Administration	127	127	37,494	10	10	822	-	-	-	137	137	38,316
Research, Development, and Operations			199,068			(973)			(2,095)			196,000
Systems Acquisition:			67,861	10	10	456	-	-	54,694			123,011
Net Discretionary	127	127	304,423	10	10	305	-	-	52,599	137	137	357,327
DEPARTMENT OF HOMELAND SECURITY	**228,178**	**225,951**	**61,125,061**	**1,624**	**2,289**	**1,278,580**	**(758)**	**(982)**	**2,454,843**	**229,044**	**227,258**	**64,858,484**
Rescission of Prior Year Unobligated Balances	[0]	[0]	[0]	[0]	[0]	[0]	[0]	[0]	[0]	[0]	[0]	[0]
Net Discretionary	199,529	199,421	44,631,533	254	396	822,161	(768)	(992)	2,452,973	199,015	198,825	47,906,667
Adjusted Net Discretionary	199,529	199,421	44,631,533	254	396	822,161	(768)	(992)	2,452,973	199,015	198,825	47,906,667
Discretionary Fee Funded	1,979	1,872	4,505,990	55	62	(465,520)	10	10	1,870	2,044	1,944	4,042,340
Gross Discretionary	201,508	201,293	49,137,523	309	458	356,641	(758)	(982)	2,454,843	201,059	200,769	51,949,007
Adjusted Gross Discretionary	201,508	201,293	49,137,523	309	458	356,641	(758)	(982)	2,454,843	201,059	200,769	51,949,007
Mandatory, Fees, Trust Funds	26,670	24,658	11,987,538	1,315	1,831	921,939	-	-	-	27,985	26,489	12,909,477

www.ingramcontent.com/pod-product-compliance
Lightning Source LLC
Chambersburg PA
CBHW052001280526
45793CB00005B/801